THRIVING DOG TRAINERS
BOOK 2

GET BETTER CLIENTS, WORK LESS, ENJOY YOUR LIFE AND BUSINESS

TED EFTHYMIADIS

Thriving Dog Trainers Book 2

Get better clients, work less, enjoy your life and business

Published by Ted Efthymiadis
Halifax NS Canada
www.tedsbooks.com

INTRODUCTION

If you have not read the first book in this series, it's called Thriving Dog Trainers and I would highly recommend reading that book before reading this one. In that book, I outlined a process that I was taught by my mentor, the process that helped me go from broke-as-a-joke to living-the-dream. If you're struggling financially as a dog trainer, I highly suggest checking that book out if you want to take your business to the next level.

This book is the continuation, in the sense that it takes those basic ideas to the next level. My mentor taught me two things in our five-year mentorship. He taught me how to be a great, open-minded dog trainer, and he taught me how to make money as a dog trainer. Before his help, I was charging my clients per hour and I was struggling because I could not keep my clients long term which meant that I was always having to find new clients to keep money coming in each month. Thriving dog trainers addressed that problem and has helped dog trainers around the world make a larger, more reliable income, and it was written with that goal in mind. If you read the first book you'll notice that again, this is not a dog training book. That book was really pointed at getting more clients and this book is focused on how to serve those clients. This book contains the lessons my mentor didn't teach me.

I wrote this book with a muse in mind. A female dog trainer who is the age of 35 years old, who owns her own business and works mainly with clients in a private setting. As you'll come to learn, much of the advice in the book is outlined for the trainers who own their own businesses because a significant portion of this book focuses on finding the right clients, a luxury that most trainers don't have if they have a boss lining up clients for them. Heaps of advice in this book are applicable to all dog trainers, regardless of gender, and age, but I want to be honest in telling you that I did not write this book for all dog trainers. I wrote this book for dog trainers who are disappointed with their new careers. The trainers who thought that being a dog trainer was going to be fun, only to have their dreams brought back to earth when they realized that working with humans can be really hard. I focus on dog trainers who are self-employed because they can pick the clients that they want to work with and mainly write to trainers who do private lessons and board and training. If you run massive group classes and don't care who signs up to your classes, this book is not for you.

In this book you'll learn more about;

- How to tell the difference between good clients VS bad clients
- How to filter out bad clients before they give you money
- How to spot red flag clients
- How to set appropriate boundaries with clients
- When to fire terrible clients
- How to step up your communication with clients
- Five lessons I wish I was taught on day one
- How to work with dog rescues
- How to tell if your potential client is ready to change
- How to resolve conflict with clients
- Why I hate board and training dogs
- How to hire awesome staff
- How to fire staff without having a panic attack

You can find Thriving Dog Trainers Book 1 here: Thriving Dog Trainers: An indispensable tool to help you start or repair your dog training business (Business books for dog trainers)

BUILDING LASTING RELATIONSHIPS
WITH YOUR CLIENTS

*U*nfortunately, dog trainers are notorious for being challenging to deal with. It's taken some time for me to grow into the roles that I now play as a dog trainer because there are so many things that I had to improve on. Before I was a professional dog trainer, I assumed that my job would focus on training dogs, and now I know how insignificant that part of my job actually is. We have to do sales, marketing, and bookkeeping, update our websites, return phone calls and emails, train dogs, and train people. Running a dog training company requires many skill sets, and it's unlikely that you are equipped sufficiently in all of these skills. Take one skill like training people, it requires patience, knowledge, experience, picking good clients, and a desire to change just to master that one skill. To be a great dog trainer and run a thriving business, you'll need to be a well-rounded person and you should know that those skills will not come overnight.

If I excel at anything it's my ability to train people. Some would suggest that I'm highly proficient as a dog trainer, but my strength is working with people. In this book, you'll learn much about picking the right clients, and at times the idea that some clients are not amazing to work with seem cold and judgmental. When you read those portions of the book you need to remember that I don't stand in judgment of these clients. I see them for what they are in that moment, well-meaning dog owners who are lacking motivation or are not ready to change. Every day I see dog trainers complain about their clients, but I know that it was never the clients' fault, it was the trainers' fault for taking the client in the first place.

After you've mastered the art of picking the right clients, you'll want to master the art of getting motivated people to love you and do what's right for their dog. Unfortunately just getting people to love you will not always result in a well-trained dog and a happy client.

The art of getting clients to bond with you and love you can be very difficult for some dog trainers because many dog trainers really don't like people and that's why they became dog trainers in the first place. If you don't like people, I would highly suggest that you are too consumed by yourself. Ask your clients about themselves, find out interesting things about them. Find out what their passion is, what lights them on fire. When you do this, you will uncover interesting things about people that you don't have an immediate affinity for. Some will tell you of their struggles with substance abuse and you can use that information to empathize with them. Some will tell you about their job that they insist is extremely boring but might be very interesting if you ask questions. Others will tell you about their adult child who has autism who is 30 years old and still lives at home. Every person is interesting if you look deep enough and ask enough questions.

Ask your clients if they grew up with dogs, if so, have them tell you about those dogs. Write down notes about the client after your lessons and take a few moments to thank God for them. I don't know anyone that does this who still would suggest they hate people. If you can't find anything redeemable about your clients, chances are that you are looking hard enough. When you uncover some interesting facts about your client, meditate on those facts. Remind yourself that you could learn some things from this client in areas that you are deficient. It seems like every day I'm asking my clients with kids for parenting advice. Simple moments like these help to create bonds that are not easily broken.

If you are still disinterested in your human clients, focus on the love that you have for their dog. Remind yourself that if you can get through to the people, you can get through to their dogs. Use your human relationships to be the catalyst that leads to the betterment of their dogs if you need to. People who work with children are known to build bonds with parents in an effort to get through to the children because they know that the parent/parents are the ones the child spends the majority of their time with. Knowing that the only way to get through to a dog is through the dogs' owners is a powerful maxim to live by.

Building lasting relationships with clients is only done when you actually care for the humans that you serve. Simple things like emailing your clients mid-week to see how they are doing with the training is an easy, free way of building a bulletproof relationship. People want to know that you care, so you should ask them questions, talk about them, and actually listen.

It might sound silly, but do what you say you are going to do. Show up on time for your lessons and be prepared. Look over the client's chart before the lesson so that you can have the client's history fresh in your mind. Give their dogs a nickname. I love giving my clients dogs nicknames, and my clients love that about me because they know that I care for their dog. Email clients to check up on their dogs; is their dog having surgery, has an injury, or is not feeling well. If you want to build lasting bonds with your clients, the only way to do it is to actually put in the work of being interested in your clients and their dogs. Many of my clients feel so indebted to me that they bring me gifts. I have had clients over for dinner with my family and ask them if they want to stay after the lesson while I roast marshmallows with my family outside on our property. These things are not lost of your clients, and they will aid you in your career in a few ways.

When your clients love you, they will forgive you when you make a mistake. Have you ever done something incredibly foolish in front of someone that truly loves you? We all have. If that person loves you, they will laugh with you, and look for a way to mentally confirm why you are still a good person. Have you ever done something foolish in front of someone that didn't like you? The person will instinctively look for those negative attributes and use them to exploit you. If you hate Donald Trump, you naturally look for the things that he's doing wrong and downplay anything that he might do that is good, in an attempt to prove to yourself that you are a good judge of character. If your clients love you, they will forgive you when you do something wrong or stupid.

When your clients love you, you'll create little advertising machines without any effort. If you help people reach the level that they desire with their dogs and they feel that you truly cared about them, they will tell other dog owners about you. Some of my clients ask me for stacks of business cards so that they can give out to people they meet, you can't buy that type of advertising and it's completely free. When I'm talking with someone who mentions that they are looking for a good mechanic, I always send them to the same place. Maxwell is the owner of the shop that I take my car to, and I send him a lot of business because he's honest, and he actually cares about me. When I walk in the door, we always chat, he asks me about the books that I'm writing, and how my family is doing before he even asks about my car. I refer to Maxwell because he does what he says he's going to do, and he cares about me. You can form those same bonds with your dog training clients and those bonds will ensure that you never have a shortage of clients.

DID you know that I help dog trainers with their businesses? If you are not yet a dog trainer and want an in-depth mentorship with me, go to: www.mangodogs.com/the-next-generation

IF YOU ALREADY HAVE A BUSINESS AND just want to come and work with me on your business for 10 days I have a program for that too! www.mangodogs.com/shadowted

GOOD CLIENTS VS BAD CLIENTS

*A*ny dog trainer that's been working professionally for more than 5 years will tell you that they are able to tell a good client from a bad client in under 2 minutes time. Experienced trainers are even able to do the same after receiving an email from a potential client. This superpower comes from nothing other than opening thousands of emails and answering thousands of phone calls from dog owners. The quicker you can learn to tell the difference, the better your life will be, so let's get into it!

Like it or not, good clients communicate in specific ways, and bad clients do too. I understand that presenting the assumption that there are good clients and bad clients might trigger someone reading or listening to this book right now. There is a difference between someone who's interested in learning and someone who's doing it out of obligation. I've been a good student at dog training seminars and a bad student in high school, so I am not unique. The difference ultimately came down to how much I wanted to learn the information being presented. To that point, I was forced to go to high school by my parents, yet I paid money and traveled hundreds or thousands of miles to go to a dog training seminar. If you don't think that there are bad clients, you haven't been around enough clients yet. I don't sit in judgment of others who I will refer to in this book as bad clients because I know that in some things I'm a bad client. The words that my car mechanic must say to his technicians when I leave his building must be colored as once again he drains my oil and it's so black that it could pass for the crude black oil covering a well drilling machine in Texas.

While the car mechanic owns a service businesses like your dog training business, the difference is that the car mechanic doesn't have to teach you anything. You drop off the car or paperwork and come back when it's done. No maintenance, no personal growth, no getting off the couch when you would rather watch television, easy stuff. Convincing someone to pay you money to give them work to do is not an easy task. The dog training business is difficult because service businesses typically make the life of the customer easier by taking the load off them, in our business, we charge our clients money and then give them work to do and that can be difficult to stomach for some dog owners.

As a general rule, I would suggest that great clients can be born and can be made. At last, the nature VS nurture argument has arrived. You can make a good client great, but I have yet to see any dog trainers make bad clients great.

THIS NEXT SECTION will illustrate the upward and downward mobility that your clients should be capable of.

Bad clients can become a good client (Yes)
Bad clients can become a great client (No)
Good clients can become a bad client (Yes)
Good clients can become a great client (Yes)
Great clients can become a good client (Yes)
Great clients can become a bad client (No)

A FEW THINGS TO note about the table above. Awesome clients can backslide if you let them, and bad clients never become awesome ones. Don't try and make an uncommitted client what you want them to be. They don't have it in them, despite how much you want them to change, never be more invested in your clients' success than they are.

Never allow your love for the client's dogs to overshadow the fact that they may live with an uncommitted owner who would rather binge watch TV shows instead of training their dogs. Hard to motivate people aren't going to change unless they have an incredibly strong reason to change which is why I work with almost exclusively aggressive dogs. Great clients either have to really want to learn about dog training and have an interest in dog training, or they have to have a lot to lose if they don't do something and do it well. I'd love to have a six-pack, but I'm not willing to put in the hours to get those abs. A six-pack would be nice to have, but it's not something that I'm going to invest time or money into because I'm at a good weight, and I have a beautiful wife who's thrilled with the way that I look.

FEW THINGS in life cannot be purchased. A great six-pack can't be bought, and to that point, neither can a well-trained dog. You can buy a housekeeper if you are lazy or busy, you can buy your groceries online and have them delivered, but you can't buy a six-pack on Amazon and you can't buy a well-trained dog. Surely you can purchase a pre-trained dog, but unless you are going to invest time into your dog, their skills will soon be lost.

IN ANSWERING what constitutes a good client, let's tweak the question slightly. If our clients are students then what makes a good student?

- A good student shows up on time or early
- A good student takes notes
- A good student is interested in what they are learning
- A good student asks questions
- A good student wants to know what to do so that they can change
- A good student brings their teacher an apple every morning

What makes a bad student?

- A bad student shows up late
- A bad student does not take notes
- A bad student is not interested in what they are learning
- A bad student does not ask questions
- A bad student wants you to do things for them
- A bad student brings their teacher a headache every morning

I DON'T KNOW about you but I would choose to spend time with a good or a great client over a bad client any day of the week. Life is too short to spend it with people that make you want to beat your head against a wall. Apart from the birth of my kids, no greater gift has been granted to me than the gift of not needing to take every client that contacts me. Being financially able to pick clients has taken my daily stress levels from off the charts to essentially non-existent. Seriously, today my largest stress-inducing moment was not a client, it was going to the refrigerator and finding that we were out of mayonnaise.

One might suggest that it's the role of the teachers, or trainer to get the students excited about what they are learning and that is partially true. Providing a fun, interactive environment for clients to learn is essential but it will not inspire a 14-year-old boy to put down his video game to go out and do the dog training homework. Never underestimate the ability of a bad client to make you want to put a gun to your head. Seriously. I'm just realistic enough to know the people that I can inspire and the ones that are going to be frustrating.

IF YOU WANT to check out my free video course for dogs trainers you can check it out here: www.tedsbooks.com/book-2-res

FILTERING OUT BAD CLIENTS
BEFORE THEY GIVE YOU MONEY

*F*inding awesome clients is much more of a science than an art. Dog trainers don't just arrive at having awesome clients, they learn to find the good clients and avoid the not so good clients. The first thing that you'll want to do is ask everyone who contacts you about your dog training services to fill out a contact form so that you can easily compile their information for later reference. If you have a website, you can integrate a contact form into your website very easily. Even if you don't have a website, the companies mentioned below will give you the ability to create a link to a form that can be emailed to potential clients or you can post the form on your website if you have one, or linked directly from your Facebook page.

A CONTACT FORM **will serve to;**
  • Hold all of your client data, which will make it easier to look up client information at a later time
  • Analyze your client data, which will make it easier for you when you are looking for basic statistics on your potential clients
  • Filter out potential clients who are not willing to take 20 minutes to fill out the form

. . .

I PERSONALLY USE Google forms for this task because I love Google products and it's free! Jotforms.com is also a good solution, but it will cost you about $10/month. Survey monkey is also a popular tool.

So WHAT SHOULD you put in this form?

• Ask the potential client for their basic information like name, phone number, email

• Ask the potential client for their dog's basic information like name, age, breed/mix, sex, weight

• Ask the potential client for information like, if their dog is up to date on vaccinations, and if they are spayed or neutered

• Ask the potential client which veterinarian they take their dog to

• Ask the potential client if they have taken their dog to any dog training previously

• Ask the potential client how often they walk their dog

• Ask the potential client how they heard about your business

• Ask the potential client if their dog has any health issues or food allergies

• Ask the potential client what their dog does that they want to change

• Ask the potential client if their dog has ever been medicated for any behavioural issues or is currently being medicated

• Ask the potential client if their dog has ever (for any reason) bitten any human

• Ask the potential client if their dog has ever (for any reason) bitten another dog

• Ask the potential client if they want to mention anything else

HERE ARE a few statistics from my website form.

. . .

- 59% of the dogs I'm contacted about are male dogs and 41% are female
  - 82% are spayed or neutered
  - 71% of the potential clients have only one dog
  - 29% are not up to date of vaccinations
  - 60% of potential clients struggle with their dog pulling on the leash
  - 72% of potential clients own dogs who are dog aggressive
  - 60% own human aggressive dogs
  - 13% have resource guarding issues
  - 34% steal food from the counters
  - 45% act like a maniac at the front door

As you can see by the data, I work with a lot of aggressive dogs. This data is beneficial to know what potential clients are struggling with so that I can provide a service that's in line with what they want help with.

I'm also mining this data for information that will keep me safe on the job. If a potential client claims that their dog has bitten 4 people on my evaluation form, I need to be on high alert and potentially suggest they buy a muzzle before I'm willing to meet with them.

The major reason that you should use one of these forms is to find out what your potential clients are hearing about you, don't forget that question because it's vital. In order for me to know how to get more awesome clients, I need to know where they came from right? And the same is true for my not so great clients. Once you have 50 or more potential clients fill out your form you'll start to see patterns. Start by looking for patterns between the owners who signed up and the ones who did not sign up. From the ones that didn't sign up, you'll want to know how they heard about you so that you can invest less time and money into those marketing channels. If a large number of people are contacting you but not signing up and they are coming from a radio ad that you're running, you'll know that it's a waste of time and money.

To that point, remember that the opposite is true. If you notice that a large percentage of people who do sign up are being referred by a specific client or veterinarian, you'll want to spend extra time preparing a thank you gift for them and personally delivering it to say thank you.

Lastly, look at all of your clients who signed up and separate the clients who were amazing to work with from the ones that were challenging. What patterns do you see? I personally get the best client referrals from past clients and so I focus on maximizing that marketing channel. I find that people who hear about me by my Facebook page almost never sign up for training and are much less committed than ones who were referred by a veterinarian. Below you'll find a simple chart showing where the most awesome clients come from. Number one produces the best clients and number twelve generally produces headaches.

1. From past clients
2. From veterinarian referral
3. From dog walker referral
4. Readers of my dog training books
5. Dog owners who have purchased one of my online courses
6. From Google
7. From Facebook
8. From the yellow pages
9. From yelp
10. From the signage in front of my facility
11. From radio interviews
12. From newspaper articles

It's easy to understand why I don't bother doing radio interviews or allow newspapers to write stories about me any longer. I've found that the amount of potential clients that they send my way is not enough to move the needle, and the clients that are generated from these forms of advertising do not tend to be committed. Knowing where your awesome clients come from and where your not so awesome clients come from is essential and I don't know many dog trainers who know the answers to those simple questions.

DID you know that I help dog trainers with their businesses? If you are not yet a dog trainer and want an in-depth mentorship with me, go to: www.mangodogs.com/the-next-generation

IF YOU ALREADY HAVE A BUSINESS AND just want to come and work with me on your business for 10 days I have a program for that too! www.mangodogs.com/shadowted

HOW TO SPOT RED FLAG CLIENTS

$\mathcal{I}$t's vital to note that when I talk with a client and I notice a red flag or warning indicator, that does not mean that I refuse to work with the client. A red flag is just a signal, think of it like driving into a new subdivision where you are going to go and look at buying a new home. If you drive into the area and see one police car in the area, your mind will take note. If you see two police cars, you might mention the cars to your spouse. If you notice 3 or 4, you are starting to reconsider the area entirely, and 5 or more cars will eliminate the neighborhood completely. Think of red flags that a client shows as police cars. One is usually ok, two is a concern, three is starting to make me rethink, four is a no, and five is just scary.

AT ODDS with their spouse

Trying to change a dog's life that's owned by a battling couple can be very difficult. Please don't assume that I will not work with a couple who is clearly dealing with relationship problems, in fact, one of the best parts about my job is when I'm able to help a couple who has conflict in their relationship. Many marriages have been saved by skilled dog trainers who are able and willing to tackle these treacherous waters, but it takes the right trainer to work that magic.

I like to start by evaluating the client's relationship with a basic relationship evaluation tool. What I do look for is the way that couples talk to each other. When couples put each other down or blame each other in front of me, I note that as being a big red flag. It's not so much about what they are saying, I'm also looking for the tone they use when they talk. It's common for me to dive deeper when I sense a toxic relationship because I need to know that they can work together instead of against each other. I've helped many couples that most trainers would turn away, suggesting that the couple was not on the same page. It's my view that most of these couples can be helped, but be cautious of the couples who clearly have contempt for each other as they often try and work against each other instead of working towards the greater goal.

Ask questions like "If I give you guys a step by step roadmap for training your dog, will you guys both follow it? If they look at each other and can collect themselves enough for a moment to be civil with each other, there is hope. If they immediately start blaming each other (men tend to do this more than women), you might want to proceed with caution. More on this topic in the topic specific to training couples. One of the most beneficial things that a dog trainer can do for a couple who is in conflict is to give them a game plan to follow, and honestly, plenty of my clients come to me hoping to get a solid game plan. One spouse might be over the moon insane about not letting their dog on the sofa, while the other spouse might let their dog on the sofa when their partner is not at home. Be diligent to define what couples should do and not do with their dogs because oftentimes the ambiguity is the biggest stress in the relationship.

WHAT WE WILL DO, *and not do*

Watch for the clients who begin the training relationship by making demands, telling the trainer what they will do and what they will not do. I don't believe that the customer is always right. When selling a product like a cell phone, it's easy to tell who is right and who is wrong. If the phone comes out of the box brand new and will not turn on, it's the manufacturer's fault. While it's easy to assume that the customer is always right in the product world, this maxim is very difficult to apply to services that rely on expert knowledge.

If you go to a restaurant for dinner, it's reasonable to tell your server that you have food allergies when ordering your meal. What's not reasonable is for you to go into their kitchen and look at every specific label on every can, and inspect the vegetables, meat, fish. I can make this analogy because I have had serious food allergies for over 15 years that will put me out of commission if I ingest just a small amount of gluten or lactose. At some point, you have to go to a restaurant that you believe will do a good job in preparing the style of dishes that you want to eat, but also dishes that will not harm you. Either your potential clients will trust you and the tools and methods that you use, or they will not. It's your job to educate them via your website, Facebook, emails, phone calls, in person meetings, so that they will know exactly how you plan to train their dog.

After educating the potential client on the tools and methods that you use, you need to leave it with them and walk away from things. They will either be into your style or not. If people refuse to use food in training because they think that it's bribery, and I educate them on the reasons why using food is going to be a benefit in the training process and the client refuses to use the methods that you are suggesting, it's often better to refer them to a more fitting trainer. Flexibility and open-mindedness are crucial when seeking new clients.

When someone asks me for help with their dog, I don't expect them to take any of my suggestions without question, but I do expect them to listen to my answer and weigh the options. I've had people refuse to use every tool and technique on the planet, and luckily for me, it's very early in our relationship, so I can pass them off to another trainer before investing more than 20 minutes into these clients. I get it, owning a dog is an emotional thing, and there are plenty of ways to train our beloved pets, but it's important for dog owners to at least hear the trainer's suggestions, ask questions, and then make a decision.

I've seen people refuse using a halti because they had a dog 20 years ago who didn't like the halti, so they refused trying it on their new dog. I've seen people refuse to use a muzzle on their dog who had bitten 5 people, because "It will make him look aggressive". Is the person who refuses to use a muzzle right or wrong? I would rather invest time with clients that are open-minded. All we're asking for is the openness to hear the trainer out, ask questions and respect their opinions, regardless of whether they take them or not. Some potential clients will never come around to your line of thinking, and some will be open-minded enough to take your suggestions based on your experience. The trick is to get a good idea which ones are open to change and which ones are not before investing weeks or months into the relationship.

DOG TRAINER HOPPERS

Some dog owners are like church hoppers. A church hopper is a Christian who goes to a new church for a few weeks, and then moves onto the next church when they don't like something about the church. It could be the music, the childcare, the sermon, whatever. Like a man or woman who can't seem to stay in a relationship for more than a few months, they always find something wrong with the other person. These people always think there's something wrong with the church, or the person they are dating and never find the self-awareness to consider that maybe they are the problem. They are hard to please, they don't want to make concessions, and they expect things to go their way without exception. Dog trainer hoppers have the same root problem, they don't want to change, they want to be told what they want to hear, and they will hop around until they find that.

One of the questions I ask in my evaluation form on my website is, have you ever worked with another dog trainer before, or is this your first time seeking training. As per my data, 64% have worked with one or more trainer in the past. So how do I separate the dog trainer hoppers from the ones who are open-minded and willing to change? The easiest way is to ask them questions, like these;

- Have you ever taken your dog to dog training before?
- How many levels of training did you do?
- How did you get along with the trainer?

- What were the names of the trainers?
- What specific things did they ask you to do with your dog?
- What specific things did they ask you not to do with your dog?
- Are you still doing any of the things they suggested that you do, or do not do?

It's in these questions where is easy to spot the dog trainer hoppers. They are easy to pin down because they typically have a few things in common.

- They typically can't even remember the first name or last name of their previous trainers
- They typically have been to at least 2 or more dog trainers
- When asked what the last trainers asked them to do and not do, they typically don't remember or have stopped doing these things that the trainer suggested

There are a lot of terrible dog trainers out there and sometimes people just waste money on a crappy trainer, but you'll want to determine the clients who have been to a lot of trainers and never took their trainers advice. If the advice they were given was terrible advice (and sometimes it is) they get a pass. If they were given solid advice from multiple trainers, and have not taken that advice, and hopped around to other trainers, it's going to be almost impossible for me to get clients to change. They don't want to change.

THEY WANT **a dog trainer who's going to tell them what they want to hear, not what they need to hear.**

IF A POTENTIAL CLIENT calls me and has been to most of the trainers in town, either they have a really hard dog that no one has been able to figure out, or the client is a dog trainer hopper. Hoping that I'll get them a six-pack without any crunches, these clients are impossible to change. It's common for me to ask these dog owners hard questions like this.

- If the last 4-5 trainers couldn't help you, have you ever taken a moment to ask yourself if you are the problem and not them?
- What are two things your previous trainer wanted you to do and two things they wanted you to stop doing? Are you still doing the things that they wanted you to do?

PARENTS BUYING *training for kids*

When a parent calls me, telling me of their child who is in their 20's or 30's is in need of help with their dog, my answer is simple and to the point. "Have them call me." They typically suggest that their son or daughter is busy at college, but struggling and in need of help. Tell your son or daughter that you did some research, found a trainer and that trainer needs you to call him, set up a time to come in to meet and at which point the trainer will guide you through how the programs work and how much it's going to cost them.

The parent thanks me for my time, tells me that they will have their son or daughter call me and that's the end of the call. In all of my years, I have yet to date had one of these kids actually call me. Not once. I understand that some parents see their kids struggling and want to help, but it's not going to help anyone if the parent is the one asking for help and the actual owner of the dog is not ready to invest time and money into training. Unless the son or daughter is willing to show up, and do the work, I refuse to take the money from the parent. If the son or daughter did not even invest enough to do the research, why would they do the training? Often I tell the parent that I will not take money from the parent either, the child needs to pay for the training because as I like to say "people take seriously what they pay for dearly."

Few dog trainers have good success with parents buying dog training for loved ones. I reached out to many other trainers and heard essentially the same sentiments. Kids not showing up for lessons, and not doing homework.

Jesus Christ said it brilliantly after the townsfolk from his hometown kicked him out of the city and tried to attack him. "A prophet is never welcome in his hometown." The advice may be more than 2000 years old, but it still rings true today.

I refuse to work with friends or family unless I'm doing it for free. As a rule, I just never do it, but if I had to make a concession to keep a family member from hating me and causing a lot of family drama, it would be done for free. Free is a good price because then they can't complain, ever. In the past, I did not heed the advice of mentors who cautioned me of this, and I had to learn this principle the hard way. Some dog trainers that I know, will work with friends and family. I reached out to one of my dog training communities and these were the findings.

- 41% do work with friends and family
- 40% do not work with friends or family but will offer them free training tips
- 19% will work with friends but not family

There are plenty of reasons why I refuse to work with friends or family.

- I don't want to jeopardize my relationship with them in any way
- Friends and family typically expect free training or a large discount and charging them a training fee can seem like a stab in the back
- Friends and family typically don't invest as much time into the training, treating their homework like it's optional
- Friends and family typically show up late for training like they might if you both were meeting for a coffee

My experience in this area has not been encouraging and thankfully rather limited, so I asked for some advice in this area and the following information was made by professional dog trainers from around the world.

Bartering for services is a great way to exchange services with friends and family rather than giving them free services. If you have a family member who plows snow in the winter or does landscaping, it might be a good trade.

Another trainer suggested giving them a 10-20% discount and assigning them to one of your trainers if you are not the only trainer in your business.

Free advice was suggested many times as a great option to give friends and family. It's my experience that many times friends and family will ask for advice and not take the advice, so keep your expectations low if you give advice and it's not used. Another option is to give friends and family a discount on your services with the expectation that they will give you a testimonial and refer you to their friends.

If you don't want to work with friends or family, referring them to another good local trainer is a great option. Remember that applying a mild disappointment by not working with a friend or family might be a lot easier for you both to get over than if you take them on and things go badly.

Can't follow orders

Today I'm lucky to have my own dog training facility, but for the first five years, I would drive to my clients and do in-home training. While I learned a lot in those years, one of the most critical things that I learned in those years was that people act very differently on their property than they do when they are on your property. For example, I would tell every potential client on the phone that when I came to their home, their dog must have a leash on before I would come inside. "Have a leash on your dog when I get there and be holding onto the leash, or have them in a crate, I'll be there at 5 pm sharp."

Most of the time people would be prepared when I got to their home, but about 10% of the time, owners would allow their dog to run-up to the door, bark at me, and then the owners would start to open the door and invite me in. I would close the door, refuse and not go in until they leash their dog.

I've walked away from homes and potential clients because they clearly care more about their dogs' freedom then they do about my safety. If someone wants my help, they have to at least play by my rules when it comes to safety. I've evaluated about 2000 dogs over the years, and fully rehabilitated about 1200, and in that time I've only been bitten once. That's only possible because I take my safety seriously. Tell the client what you need them to do before you come to their homes, and if they don't follow your instructions, do not go inside until they take your advice. If they will still not listen, just walk away. More on the topic of safety in the chapter that focuses on communication with clients.

CHEAP PEOPLE

The day that you realize you don't have to be everything for everybody, your life will start to become less stressful. Regardless of how much money you charge your clients, you'll always have some clients suggest that your prices are too expensive. You can charge $200 to change someone's life, or $2000 and you'll still get people moaning about the price. The difference is that the $2000 clients will moan a lot less, do a lot more work, refer a lot more clients, and generally do a better job. More on this topic in the pricing chapter. Cheap people like to moan about pricing. They often will be on your website, looking at your prices, while talking to you on the phone when they ask you what your prices are. They already know how much you charge, but they just want to bellyache about your prices.

When my phone rings, I'm always upbeat when I say "Ted the dog trainer, how can I help you?" Typically the person I'm talking with will start to tell me about their dog and how problematic he/she is. The cheap people do not ask about my methods, my programs, my experience, the first thing that they talk about is the price. If the person directly asks about pricing, I refer them to a more economical trainer.

Well, that seems a little drastic, doesn't it? Surely it does and it is drastic, but I have never, after roughly 5000 phone calls, had one call that focused on price that actually turned into a good client. If you do more basic services like basic obedience classes, the idea is the same. It's common for dog owners to call around for those classes and try and get the cheapest price, but I don't know if you want the ones who call and ask for a price before they even tell you their name.

What is totally acceptable in my opinion is when someone calls, tells me about their dog, asks me questions, asks for help, and then asks about the price. What throws up a red flag for me is when they persist on price and don't care about anything else. One line emails saying "Hey, how much do you charge?" are not expected to yield a great client.

REALLY LONG EMAILS

All dog trainers get a lot of emails, and anyone who's been at the trade for a while will tell you that short emails are bad, and typically very long emails including a photo of their dog are really bad. Early in my career, I was so excited by these long emails until I started to see a theme. These emails include a long history of their dog, a photo of their dog, and a plea for help. 75% of the time these emails also have a classic line that all dog trainers hate. "We don't have much money, but we love our dog". These crazy long emails almost never produce a client, they are however a way for the dog owner to convince themselves that they've done everything for their dog before rehoming or putting them down. When replying to these emails, I will thank them for their detailed email and photo and suggest that we meet to talk about some training programs and pricing and I only receive an email reply back about 5% of the time.

This enigma used to both fascinate and frustrate me, and now after receiving over 500 of them, I just send the reply and don't expect to ever hear back from them. Six weeks ago I had a nice young women call me pleading for help with her pit bull mix. She went on to tell me that her 3.5-year-old male pittie mix needed help because he was very aggressive. I listened and sympathized for about 10 minutes and then I suggested that she and her partner should bring their dog in for an evaluation. She said she would look at her partner's schedule and get right back to me. Five weeks passed and I didn't hear back from her.

Then I got an email from her that was several pages long and included a photo of her dog. Nowhere in the email did she offer any times that she and her partner could come in and meet. So I emailed her back thanking her for the email and photo and suggested that she send over some times and dates, and again no response. It was like she had just sent the email to every dog trainer in the area then deleted her email account. She did not even reference our phone conversation six weeks prior.

Don't invest a significant amount of time or energy into these email responses because their goal is almost never to sign up to dog training, it's more of an exercise in journaling for them.

IF YOU WANT to check out my free video course for dogs trainers you can check it out here: www.tedsbooks.com/book-2-res

HOW TO SET APPROPRIATE
BOUNDARIES WITH CLIENTS

The vast majority of dog trainers that I know became dog trainers because they thought that they would be working with dogs all day. As you've likely already figured out, that's not the case. In working with dogs, two things are abundantly clear, they don't have credit cards and they will need ongoing support from their owners if they are going to thrive. When working with humans, appropriate boundaries need to be set into your daily business and personal life to ensure that you don't find yourself becoming frustrated when a client does something that you find frustrating.

People will treat you the way that you allow them to treat you.

Over the years I've met several dog trainers who unfortunately shut down their businesses and left the industry for reasons that could have been entirely avoided. These dog trainers all struggled to set proper boundaries. This gray area in which tension lives and resentment breeds can be found camped out right next to a river known as the things I should have said but didn't.

With boundaries, it's not what you say that gets you in trouble; it's what you don't say. We all have those feelings from time to time when we mentally are pissed off at ourselves because we know that we are being taken advantage of, yet we also know that it's just as much our fault as it is our clients' fault. The good news is that I can't remember a time when I clearly drew a line in the sand and it was clearly disrespected.

Short term awkwardness is better than long term discomfort.

Make it part of your website, emails, and phone calls to properly communicate your boundaries with clients and potential clients so that they know what to expect and I think you'll find it a rare thing to have them disrespect your boundaries. Starting your relationship early with communication about boundaries is important because it will set you apart as a professional. Nothing reeks of amateur more than loosely defined expectations.

While I believe that there are some naughty clients out there in the world, I know that it's almost always brought on by the trainer not setting the proper boundaries at the beginning of the relationship. The thing about relationships is that it's really hard to change boundaries when you are in the middle of a relationship because boundaries typically get worked out in the earliest part of any relationship. Changing boundaries mid relationship is always going to cause a significant amount of resentment and awkward conversations.

Let me tell you a story that clearly illustrates the importance of setting proper boundaries from the very onset. A woman called me, asking for help with her German shepherd about three weeks ago. I talked to her for about 15 minutes, assured her that I could help her out and I booked a time for her to come in for an evaluation the following week. I got her the first available time slot because she was very concerned about her dog's aggressive behaviour. Two days later, I got a call from my wife who was outside in our backyard. "Hey babe, there's a woman here who wants to talk to you, can you come out for a sec?"

I told my wife that the woman would have to wait in her car until I was ready to come outside. At the time, I was writing this book and do not allow distractions when I'm hard at work, focusing on a book. I was close to finishing a chapter, so I finished the chapter, put on my shoes and went out to see who had come by and wanted to see me as this is a very rare situation in my life. To my surprise, it was the woman who I had talked to 48 hours earlier about her German shepherd. She wanted me to talk with her right away. I was nice to her, but

I assured her that she was going to need to leave and come back at the appointed time.

My loving heart wanted to sit down with the lady, take a look at her dog and give her some quick advice, but I knew deep down that if I had done that, I would have been enabling her pushy behaviour. Normal human beings don't make a doctor's appointment, and then just show up and demand to see the doctor. This woman was allowing her emotions to override her common sense. She could have called me, she could have emailed me, but she chose to show up, unannounced, hoping that I would feel sorry for her. Sure I felt sorry for her, but I knew that if I dropped my writing at that moment, I would have missed my writing goal for the day and I also knew that I would have been reinforcing this woman's manipulation attempt.

The same day, she emailed me and said that her dog was going to be staying with her ex-boyfriend for a while and that she would get back to me to set up another time to meet, which she never did. I dodged a bullet. Some might suggest that she really needed help and that I turned her away when she was overwhelmed and that sentiment would likely be true. But it's not my job to fix everyone's problems the moments they want them fixed. This woman was disrespectful in her approach to getting help and likely that she would have been a terrible client.

Let me break down what I did with this woman in that 30-second meeting, with the hope that you can also implement some of these techniques.

- I didn't go directly outside to talk to the woman, I made her wait until I was ready to go outside
- I didn't give in to her appeal for immediate attention, I told her she would have to come back at the time that we had agreed on
- I didn't allow her emotional appeals to change my day, and potentially take on a very unstable client
- I set up a proper boundary by holding my ground, that would have made it abundantly clear how I allow people to

treat me and my time if we did end up working together in the future

I would never judge this woman for the way that she acted, but I do need to be realistic in assuming that if she's going to start the relationship with manipulation, it's very likely that she will try the same in the future. Given the fact that she never called me back, I can only assume that she did appreciate how firm I was on my rules and I'm so happy that I did not bend to her hostage-taking attempt over my morning.

TEXTING *with clients*

It was 1:50 am when I turned over in my bed to grab my phone off the nightstand. My phone was buzzing which was a very rare occurrence at that time given the hour of the night. My wife also woke up and asked me if there was an emergency. I told her that it was nothing and she went back to sleep. As I lay awake in my bed at 1:51 am, I remember all these years later, asking myself why any human being would send their dog trainer a text message of their dog playing in a mud puddle at 1:50 am in the morning.

In the morning I had some time to think on the previous night's events and I made the conscious choice to start telling every one of my hundreds of clients that they could not text me for any reason because it was starting to become a problem in my life. Let's unpack what texting is, and then look at some methods we can prevent texting from becoming a boundary issue with clients. Texting is;

- A method of communication
- A quick method of communication
- A quick method of communication that people expect a response from ASAP
- Apart from Morse code, it's the worst way to communicate with another human being because it's so emotion and tone deficient

Texting is the easiest way to miscommunicate with a client of any communication method because of the reasons listed above. Its speed allows for more typos and less thought given to the messages and its lack of emotion makes it an easy way to miscommunicate.

I do not text with clients. Every potential client is told when we meet that I don't text message, and not to even try because I have a flip phone, and the texting feature is turned off. Most of them laugh and then I pull out my phone and show them my phone, to which most are a little stunned. Many ask me how I ditched my Smartphone for a flip phone three years ago, and I tell them the story about the text with the photo of the dog in the mud puddle. Immediately they know that I'm serious about living a life that is not full of constant technology disruption and that I'm a professional.

Because I don't text, I reached out to a group of dog trainers to ask them why they text with clients;

- Talking on the phone produces stress for many dog trainers, so they prefer email or texting
- They like the quick ability to send off a text instead of taking the time to talk to someone on the phone.
- They like the ease of use to take photos and video to send quickly to clients if they have board and train dogs in for training
- 55% of dog trainers text with clients and love it
- 33% of dog trainers text with clients but only during regular business hours
- 12% of dog trainers don't text with clients

So, you're probably not as extreme as I am, but what are some ways to cut down or unplug from texting with clients? I know several dog trainers who have an extra phone that they pay for each month that is only for texting and calls from clients. They turn it on at 9 am and turn it off at 6 pm. I had no idea but it was also brought to my attention that there are apps that you can download for your phone to automatically respond to text messages that are received after hours. I can see how one of these apps would be a great solution for trainers who want to continue to text with clients but want to have some balance when they are not working.

Whatever you decide on the texting with clients' issue, just know that you should communicate your expectations with your clients before they start training so that you don't need to remedy a client who abuses the privilege of texting with their trainer.

I'm a real stickler for people being on time for lessons, so much so that in my evaluation forms it reminds people multiple times. Remember, if I don't take my time seriously, people will start to take advantage. If I have a potential client or client show up late; things are about to get awkward. Typically, they will get out of their cars and say, "I'm so sorry I was late, we just ran into some traffic." To which I might say, ok, it's your first time and your last time. Just leave earlier next time and we won't have a problem.

What they are expecting is for me to be a nice guy and say something like "Oh, it's ok, these things happen." The problem with saying something like that is that if I don't call them out on being late, it's much more likely that they will show up late again. If they are late once and you call them out politely, it's almost unheard of to see those people ever be late again. When you don't say something, you are allowing their lack of respect for your time, and dramatically increase the likelihood that they will be late in the future.

There are many things that you can say when someone is late, but it's much better to just pre-educate your clients about your expectations before having to call them out for being late. When I meet with a potential client, I will call them out if they are late. During the evaluation, I will also tell them if they sign up to one of my programs, last-minute cancellations or being late are not tolerated. Each of these people go home from that evaluation with a price quote sheet, and on that sheet, it says in bold letters "Being late, or last-minute cancellations will really piss off your dog trainer, so don't even try it."

You'd think that something like this would cause a decrease in people signing up, but people actually love it. They know that I'm busy, and they know that I respect my time; I'm a professional, not an amateur. If you start to become friends with one of your clients, these lines can easily start to get blurry. If this happens you can remind those client/friends via email about their session coming up, and remind them not to be late. Being late to a friend's place is almost a given, but if it's on your business time, you are losing money.

In-home trainers rarely have to deal with late clients, and I can't understand why this is. In 5 years of training dogs in their owners' homes, I think I arrived at a client's home only three times before the client got home. For whatever reason, dog owners seem to be very diligent about being home at the correct time but are less respectful if they need to drive to a group class, or your dog training facility.

Fully presenting the extent of changes your client will need to make in their lives is paramount when meeting with new clients. When I was first starting out as a dog trainer, I tried to make the training demand more palatable for potential clients. These days I actually do what I call anti-sales which is essentially playing hard to get with clients during an evaluation. Because I work with so many dogs with histories of aggression, I can't be signing up people who are not committed to changing their dog's life and doing the homework that I give them to do with their dog. It's common for me to tell potential clients things like "You're going to have to change every-thing about the way that you live with your dog, are you up for that?" Or "This is a very long term training process; you could end up having to train your dog for the rest of their lives, are you ok with that?"

I don't take money from people on the spot, I tell them to go home, think about it, pray about it, fight about it, and call me in a few days if they want to sign up. This is done for several reasons:

- It shows that you are not needy, those who are not needy are seen as sought-after

- It shows that I respect them enough to not push them into a sale
- It's a great way to build instant trust, I tell people to go home and do what is right for them and their dog, and if they want a referral to another trainer I would be glad to give them some recommendations
- It's done to avoid someone calling me in 48 hours who has buyer's remorse and wants to cancel their training program

If you work more basic obedience or puppy classes, it's not important that you play hard to get because it may cost you a lot of potential students. The hard to get sales approach is only beneficial for trainers who are working with clients with dangerous dogs, or dogs that are going to need long-term training.

DID you know that I help dog trainers with their businesses? If you are not yet a dog trainer and want an in-depth mentorship with me, go to: www.mangodogs.com/the-next-generation

IF YOU ALREADY HAVE A BUSINESS AND just want to come and work with me on your business for 10 days I have a program for that too! www.mangodogs.com/shadowted

FIRING CLIENTS

I'm not an expert in firing clients because I can only remember having to fire two clients over the last decade. It pains me to see fellow dog trainers firing so many clients. I have several dog training forums online and so I see dog trainers from around the world who fire an alarming amount of clients.

It starts even before they contact you. Your reputation is something that people will talk about over the phone, in pet stores, in dining rooms over a nice family dinner and of course on the internet. The way that you present yourself, and more importantly, the way that you act, is fundamental in having the right people contact you in the first place. In my area, I'm known for two things. I work with the tough dogs that most other trainers won't go near, and I say it like it is. With me, I'm going to tell you the truth 100% of the time. Telling people the truth is not easy but it's important and I'm known in my area for having that trait.

If I think that a potential client has a dog that is far too much dog for them, I'll straight up tell them that. If a dog owner calls me and wants my opinion on something training related I'll tell them what I think. That reputation for straight-up advice slowly starts to get around and before you know it, people talk about you like you are a person who is chock-full of integrity. I'm not always right, and I'm

33

definitely not perfect, but I am honest with people and people appreciate that.

My Facebook page is a great asset for weeding out bad clients who don't want to hear the truth. I'm very honest when blogging on Facebook and people either love or hate that. I'm ok with people not liking my upfront style because if they can't even deal with the truth over the internet, it's impossible to expect that I will be able to get them to change or stomach my views in real life. Be who you are, write or speak the truth, and try not to sound like you are better than others when you do such things. Often I tell stories about things that I did wrong with my dogs in the past as a way to illustrate that I'm not only pointing the finger at other dog owners, but I was like them. The tone that you use when being honest is the key to either looking arrogant and judgmental or looking understanding and concerned.

I was always taught by my mentor to have business cards ready to hand out to people. If I was at a pet store, buying some dog food, I was supposed to give out my cards to people who had a dog that was acting unruly. It didn't take long for me to stop that frustrating endeavor when I figured out that many of those people were offended that you even thought their precious dog was anything but perfect. Really I can't blame them, it would be like if my daughter was having a difficult time controlling her emotions at the grocery store and some guy or gal walked up to me and handed me a card, suggesting that I was a bad parent. What a low blow. I'm already humiliated, just leave me alone. I do not offer advice to dog owners unless they directly ask me for advice.

When clients want to refer me to friends or family I suggest that they don't offer to refer me unless the person has specifically asked them for a dog trainer referral. In that case, I suggest the client tells the dog owner to go to my website, do a little research and if they like what they see, to give me a call. This little step helps to weed out many dog owners that are not yet at the point where they are ready to make a large financial/time commitment. If you are an obedience trainer, your standards are probably going to be much lower for who you want to contact you, so you can leave that step out.

If a potential client calls me, I will chat with them for about 10-15 minutes to answer their questions. Most often, they want to know about the methods that I use, how long the training process will take, and a rough estimate about what the price will be. If they are still interested after our discussion, I will send them to my website and suggest that they fill out my evaluation form so that I can get their basic information into my system. I then contact them via email or phone to set up a time for them to come in to meet with me for an evaluation.

If I have them come in for an evaluation, it's required that if they have a spouse, their spouse must also come to the evaluation. For many years I did not insist on having both spouses present, and it was a pain when I would invest an hour or two into potential clients by meeting with them, and they would go home and their spouse would tell them they could not sign up.

If the occasion arises where I am meeting with a potential client and I don't like being around them, I do a few things. This is one of the most difficult things to do because it's awkward. You don't want to tell them to their face, but you also have a strong feeling that you don't think they will be a good fit with you. Call me crazy, but I don't take every client that asks for service. Life is too short to spend time with people that you don't like.

A few years ago I had a young woman call me asking for help with her human aggressive Great Pyrenees. She seemed lovely over the phone, but we did not hit it off when she came down to meet with me. Her dog was clearly a fearful dog and had bitten several people, so I was watchful to give the dog a lot of space. When her dog had relieved his blatter on 50 different parts of my property, I suggested we go inside my facility to chat. When he got to the door, the dog didn't want to go in. I've seen this a few times before, so I gave them plenty of time and space. After waiting for about 5 minutes, I suggested that she might not want to be stroking her dog and soothing him. She didn't like that request. I told her to go up to her car, and I opened my big garage door slowly as to not scare her dog. She tried to get him into the facility that way and he still was not going in, despite her praise and liver treats. I asked her if I could try and she declined my offer, so I took some chairs, put them outside in my driveway, and we sat down to talk.

The entire discussion was miserable. She was defensive to the most basic of questions and clearly, I was not her cup of tea. After a few minutes, I suggested she should find another trainer that was going to be a better fit for her. She drove away and I never heard from her again. She didn't email me as she had said she would, for a list of other trainers she should contact. Would it have helped either of us for me to have continued that conversation? Of course not!

When it's clear that the client does not like you, or your process, it's easy to suggest they go elsewhere. It's not so easy when you can't stand being near someone who fully wants to be around you. These situations are difficult because you have to somehow convey to the person that it's not a good fit, without hurting their feelings. Unrequited love is a bummer for the unloved person.

A few years ago I had a couple come in with their human aggressive dog. The female owner sounded like an angel over the phone, but as I was about to learn, her husband was very problematic. At the time I had two trainers from Oregon with me who were shadowing me for 10 days and they were with me as we met the owners at their car. The husband wanted to let their dog run around off-leash on my property which is when I knew we were going to have a big problem. A few days earlier his dog had bitten someone at the park when he was off-leash so I told him that he was not allowed to let his dog off-leash on my property. As we sat down to chat, he mentioned several times that his dog wanted to run around, and to my amazement, he starting to unclip the leash. I had to stop him several times and remind him that he was not to do that because I was concerned that his dog would bite one of us. After about 15 minutes he was getting very frustrated so I decided to address the situation. I told him that his dog's freedom was not as important as the safety of my shadow students and my own safety. If he did not want to adhere to my rules, he would have to leave.

After another 15 brutally awkward minutes, the couple left and we all let out a sigh of relief. To my shock, the next day his wife called me and apologized for her husband's behaviour and said that they wanted to sign up. I didn't even know what to say. Out of sheer desperation, I told her that unless her husband called me to apologize I would not even consider taking them on as clients and that even then I would be very apprehensive. He never called.

We just discussed a few ways to avoid taking money from problematic people who are not ready or willing to change. As a rule, honesty is a good policy, coupled with an offer to give them a list of other trainers. When you take a bad client, one that makes your head hurt, you will be faced with a choice. You can either continue to help the clients and learn from the situation, or you can fire the client.

As mentioned earlier I have only ever fired two clients, one such story is coming up shortly. Generally, I continue to work with the client as it helps me learn better how to deal with conflict and practice my own patience. Sure it's inconvenient to work with clients who are lazy, or full of excuses, but it's actually really important for dog trainers to work with these clients every once in a while so that we can be better educators of humans. I worked with countless "less than savory" clients in the first 4-5 years of business because I had a wedding to fund and I wanted to help my wife pay off her student loans. Nothing like financial goals to get a guy to deal with a lot of headache-inducing clients who make the process difficult.

As a rule, if I take on a client I don't fire them unless they tell an egregious lie to me that can't easily be forgiven or put me in a very unsafe situation. The following is a story about the first of two clients that I have fired.

On October 12th, 2014 I got a call from a woman who had a greyhound she needed some help with. As she unraveled her dog's history of dog aggression I stopped her mid-sentence when she told me that she had a greyhound. I asked her which rescue she adopted her dog from, but in my heart, I already knew. The only local greyhound rescue has very strict rules for their adopting families. These dogs are never allowed off-leash unless in a fenced-in yard and have to be muzzled for their entire lives. If any training tool apart from a front clip harness is used in their training, they will take your dog away from you.

Knowing that this rescue makes their adopters sign a contract with these stipulations, I suggested to the women that she should try and find a more fitting trainer. I'm all for trying to help people use whatever tools they want, but I can't get a dog to be off-leash around other dogs by only using a front clip harness. She told me that they must have changed their contract because those training stipulations were not in her contract. I told her to find the contract and call me back. Twenty minutes later she called me back and told me that she was looking at the contract and that they must have changed their stance on training. Stupidly I believed her. A much wiser choice would have been to call the rescue instead of blindly believing her, or I could have asked her to email me a copy of the contract.

We met a week later for an evaluation, she was comfortable with the tools, methodology, and price and wanted to sign up on the spot, so I told her to go home and think about it for a few days. She called back a few days later to get booked in.

The first lesson was like most others for the first 30 minutes, I started to get a feel for her dog, just working with him on a slip leash/longline and some food. Then something shifted in the dog. At one point, the longline was under one of his legs and he looked back at me as if to say, come over here and get this longline sorted out and I'll take your handoff. I'm pretty good at reading body language, so I decided to stop the lesson and ask if she had his muzzle with him. She did not have his muzzle, so I told her to go home and we would continue with her dog the following week with the muzzle. She insisted that he was in no way human aggressive, which she mentioned during our first phone call and our in-person evaluation. This time I trusted my gut and not her word. I ended the lesson and told her to come back with the muzzle and we would continue.

Wednesday at 3 pm the following week her car pulled into my driveway. As I walked up my driveway to greet my client and her dog I noticed not just one woman in the car but three. A pleasant older women shook my hand and greeted me with a big smile when they exited the car. Another woman (the clients sister) shook my hand, and then drove into something that can only be referred to as a verbal smackdown, you know, the kind you might see on the Jerry Springer show when someone enters the stage to confront their baby-daddy who hasn't paid child support in 5 years. "You unethical piece of crap, you took money from my sister, all the time knowing that this dog is not supposed to be trained with any form of correction, you piece of crap… blah blah blah. " Surprisingly at that moment, I felt a calm come over my body because I knew that I had done nothing to deserve the verbal assault, so I thanked her for coming and suggested that we go inside to talk. Mother and two daughters sat down on the sofa in my facility and things were feeling weird. They left their dog in the car, (don't worry the weather was cool and the windows were rolled down slightly) the client is looking at me like she's in trouble, the mother is now mortified, and the sister wants to kill me and throw my body in a river.

Calmly, I ask the sister to tell me what's going on, so that I can understand why she's so upset with me. The client's sister was convinced that I had somehow forced her sister into using training techniques that she was not allowed to under her signed contract. She thought that I was jeopardizing the relationship that her sister had with her dog because her dog might be taken from her if someone discovered that she was my client. I addressed the room by saying, "Actually your sister told me that she had not signed such a contract, and I even suggested that she check her contract, so someone seems to not have all of the facts". The sister of the client turned an even deeper shade of red as she looked over at her fibbing sister with disdain. Their sweet mother caught in the middle of the couch trying to end a nuclear war between sisters.

After watching the two murder each other with words, I stood up and told them both to knock it off. They simmered down and I was able to talk. "Ok, here's the deal. Your sister lied to me, that's all that I know. She told me that her dog was dog aggressive and needed some training so I decided to try and help them." The client's sister then let me in on some useful information that I didn't know. She told me that the dog had a muzzle order not just because it was mandatory with the rescue but because our local animal control applied one on her dog after he killed a small dog at a local park. She then went on to tell me that this dog had bitten several people including the sister twice. I thanked the sister for the information, went over to my office supply cabinet, got out my checkbook and wrote the client a check for the full amount that she paid me. "Take this check, leave right now, and I never want to see your face ever again, goodbye." Now you know what it takes for me to fire a client.

Do I fire clients for being late? No. Do I fire clients for being less than committed to training? No. Will I fire clients for canceling? No. The only thing that I will fire a client for is the act of lying to me, especially if it put myself or my dogs in danger. The fact is that I've had plenty of bad, unmotivated, uncommitted clients over the years, but I don't fire them, because I'd rather learn from them. So what can you learn from these types of clients? As we've discussed, I've learned who I can and cannot change, and that knowledge has decreased the stress in my life by 90%. It's so incredibly rare that I have a client now that I don't love to be around, or that isn't doing a good job with the training. I bring the right types of people into my life and don't allow the wrong types into my life. In those early years I would take on anyone as a client because I needed the cash, I wanted to work with as many dogs as humanly possible, and because I thought I was a super-hero who could change people. In those years I also learned that it's my fault when I take money from someone who doesn't end up being a good client, and with that in thought, can I blame the person for my actions? Instead of fire clients, I study my patience and make notes about the clients so that I can learn to catch these red flags in the future.

Training dogs is a lot like dating. You get to know what you like, and what you don't. Most don't marry the first person they date. After dating a few people you should know better things to look for in the next relationship, but it's very hard to find out these desires until you are in a relationship. Like dating, we can learn from past clients what to look out for in future ones. Remember that if you show your clients how you expect to be treated and properly communicate your expectations, it's very unlikely that you will have issues with clients and need to think about firing them.

When I asked a group of dog trainers why they fire clients, the reasons included;

• The client is always late

40

- The client has canceled several lessons
- The client is not doing the homework that I suggested
- The client is not comfortable with the tools or methods that I typically use

WHEN I LOOK at this list, I see problems that are completely avoidable. Did you tell potential clients that you can't have people showing up for lessons late because it completely throws off your day and will limit how much time you get to spend with them? Did you give the clients printed homework instructions to follow that are easy to implement for the client? Did they know what was expected from them before they started the training? Did they know what tools you would be using? Did they know the time commitment each day, and for how long?

If you can honestly say that you did a great job at communicating all of these themes to your client before starting training and they still are not doing the work, here is a little trick that my mentor taught me that I use about once a year. If the client cancels a lesson, I will remind them that we discussed you only get one cancellation which needs to be 48 hours in advance. After that cancellation, I put them on a call and see plan. By call and see, I mean they need to call me on the day that they want to come in, and I will see if I have time to meet with them. The committed clients will call you and do what they can to get in for a lesson on short notice. The clients who don't care, will likely just fizzle out and you'll never hear from them again. You need to properly communicate with these clients how much time they have access to your private services. This time crunch is essential so that clients don't call you 3 years later demanding to meet with you.

Upfront I tell my potential clients how many lessons they can expect, what happens if they are late, or cancel, and how long they have access to me. If they don't put in the work, they are wasting their money. If I have a client who does not do the homework, I put a small roadblock in front of them. If several weeks in a row the client is not putting in the work, I will tell them that I'm not going to book their next lesson just yet. They need to do something before I book their next lesson. For example, if the client has been training their dog to walk on the leash without pulling, I'll tell them that they need to walk their dog twice a day, once in the morning and once in the evening. They need to email at the end of the week with some specifics. How long each walk was. How many dogs and people they saw on each walk. How their dog did on each walk and so on. Then tell them that they can call me and book their next lesson after one week of that training and after they send me the email.

This tiny roadblock is enough to stall most uncommitted people and many will never call you again. I know how terrible this sounds because it sounds like I'm trying to get people to quit and in some ways that's true. But it's not as though I didn't tell people that they were going to have to walk their dogs twice a day. They knew what the homework was before they signed up. You'll never get every client to do a brilliant job, you're not a superhero. The idea behind this roadblock concept is just to slightly tweak the relationship so that instead of booking their next lesson each week, you make them do something that requires time and effort before they can book their next lesson. When you put up a tiny roadblock and a client can't invest that time or effort after they were told at the beginning of the relationship what to expect, they will feel as though they wasted their time and money and not pass the blame on to you.

I tell all of my clients that my door is always open, but if you show me that you're only willing to give me 50% of your time and energy, I'm going to make you show me that you are committed.

REFUNDS

Everyone has different ideas on what they should do about refunds. If you've done a great job telling people that you don't provide exchanges or refunds for any reason, and it's in the training contract that they signed, you'll rarely get someone asking for a refund. You can tell people that your training is like buying a pass to a yoga class, if you don't show up, you don't get a refund and you certainly don't get any results.

My general thought is that if a person asks for a refund, it's probably best to return their money as damage control. Knock on wood; I've only had one client ask for a refund. We worked it out with a conversation, and it came to light that this client had a lot of other things going on in her life at the time.

As the old saying goes "One unhappy customer makes more noise than 1000 happy customers". I'd much rather just part ways, rather than fight over some money. It's not worth the level of stress that it's going to produce in my life or having a potentially angry customer that's talking badly about my business.

This presents a moral problem for some dog trainers. Many of the trainers that I know refuse to give a refund because they see it as an injustice. "I worked with that client, and they are the problem, they don't deserve a refund, I can't get the time back that I wasted with those people..." This sentiment is not lost on me, as I can see and understand that outlook, but still my advice is to cut a check and move on, better prepared to spot such a problematic client in the future before they give you money. Is it worth it to refuse a refund for $1000 when that client could potentially cost you $100,000 if they really feel slighted? Try and work things out with people instead of holding hard and fast to this rule.

How your prices will change how people treat you

After providing business coaching to dog trainers around the world, one issue that stands out is that the majority of dog owners don't know how to create dog training programs, and they really struggle to price those programs. My first book, 'Thriving Dog Trainers' does a good job of laying out different dog training business models and it gives guidance on how much to charge for your services. It's for that reason I won't focus on that task in this book. It is, however, very important to understand the direct relationship between how much you charge your clients and the effort that your clients invest into training.

Surely great clients come in all shapes, sizes and price points. Some amazing clients have insignificant budgets and are willing to work hard and do a great job. Some terrible clients are wealthy and don't mind throwing money at the problem in an aim to fix things without investing time or effort. So rather than over-generalize people and price points, I'd like to unpack the major reason why I don't charge average prices. Price indicates quality. Have you ever been at a gas station and looked at the three different gasoline options and wondered what is so great about the most expensive gasoline? If you have, you just proved my point. The fact that we expect the more expensive gasoline to be of higher quality solely based on its price is not an insignificant fact.

If your prices are half that of your local competition, you will get the price shopping clients who can be much more problematic clients. If your prices are twice that of your competition, you get people calling you who are serious about having the best of the best. Average prices attract average clients, and high prices attract dedicated clients.

One of my friends who is a dog trainer is terrified of increasing his prices. He's constantly moaning about his uncommitted clients, and I keep telling him that it's because his services are so inexpensive. He's been avoiding raising his prices for years because he's afraid that he will lose potential business when in reality he has everything to lose by not raising his prices.

• His low prices make him look like an average dog trainer at best.

• His low prices attract uncommitted clients who want to cut corners

• His low prices make it hard for people to respect him, because his prices do not demand or promote respect

HIS LOW PRICES are not only keeping him in poverty, but they are forcing him to have to say yes to every client that contacts him because he needs the money so badly. Face your fear, provide a mind-blowing service for your clients, raise your prices, and enjoy your life with awesome clients.

I focus on solving people issues when creating dog training programs. I have programs to address pulling on the leash. I have programs that focus on producing reliable recall. I have programs for rehabilitating aggressive dogs. Why these programs you might ask?

Because people want to enjoy their walks again. People want to take their dogs off-leash and trust that they will come back when called. People want to know that when the UPS driver drops off a package, their dog will not try and bite them. Solve problems for people and you'll never run out of clients.

Do you provide a need or a want?

As a general rule, money is a good indicator to show how important something is to someone. Money is no object if my child is sick and the only possible solution is to fly her to Germany to undergo an untested medical procedure that could make her well. This is the way most dog owners feel about taking their dog to the vet. If I take my dog to the vet, they will fix the issues, I will make sure my dog gets his two pills a day and in a few weeks he'll be fine. As dog trainers we need to look at our businesses and ask ourselves if we provide needs or wants. In almost all cases, needs can demand a much higher premium over wants. Let's unpack some needs and wants in the dog training industry.

Wants:
- Agility training
- Basic obedience training
- Tracking and sport work
- Puppy training

NEEDS:
- Behavioural problem training
- Aggression and reactivity training

ON THE WHOLE, clients who *want* dog training are much less invested when placed next to clients who *need* to do training. Typically clients invest more effort when they have something to lose instead of something to gain. Take the client who's doing puppy classes because they want to tell themselves that they have done everything they can do to help their new puppy have a good life. When we put that same client next to a client who just adopted a dog from a local shelter who could lose their new dog if they don't finish their training course, we start to notice more urgency.

I much prefer to work with clients who have much to lose. Clients who avoid going on walks because their dog is so bad; Clients who own dogs who are out of control, or who may lose their best friend if they don't do something soon. Of course this is just personal preference, but I find that when clients stand to lose something, they invest more time into training, and do a better job than the clients who do training because they think it would be fun.

People feel the need to get the most out of something that they have paid their hard-earned money to purchase. This is a simple matter of life, and considering that both you and I are educators, we should take note of this information. This is not to say that a client that you help for free is not going to do the work, but the chances are much lower.

In 2013 I was contacted by a local veterinarian who wanted me to run puppy and basic obedience classes in their clinic. I thanked the vet for the opportunity and told him that I didn't have time to take on any classes. What I really was thinking is, sorry but you couldn't pay me a million dollars to run your classes because I know how unmotivated the clients are going to be. He asked me if I knew anyone that might be interested in the opportunity, and I told him that I would ask around and get back to him. My friend Derek was at the time working a full-time job and wanted some extra income so that he could buy his first house, I offered the position to him because he had been training part-time with me for a while.

I told him that I would help him out with the classes for a few weeks to help him get going, but I warned him that clients were paying $120 for the classes and would likely be very unmotivated to do the work. My worst fears were validated on day one. Each member of the class was sent an email with a checklist two weeks before the class was to start, and the staff at the clinic called each dog owner before the class started to ensure that they knew what was expected from them before the classes started. The first lesson went reasonably well, but only about 60% of the dog owners brought food for their dogs and made sure to bring their dogs hungry. The second week was terrible. Most of the students didn't do the homework and even fewer students brought food and a hungry dog on that night. Things progressively went downhill from there.

In analyzing the deplorable classes, I was able to determine that most of the participants were much less focused on having a great dog, and more focused on getting a certificate at the end of the classes so that they can show their friends and family. The certificate kept people coming each week, despite their lack of interest in the information. The other thing of note was that some of the clients wanted the certificates because they had recently adopted their dog from a local shelter and obedience training was mandatory in adopting their new dog.

This brings us back to the discussion on needs and wants. Some of these clients needed the certificate to appease the animal shelters that they had adopted from. Others wanted the certificate so that they could show their friends and family, or because they thought it would be a nice thing to do with their dog. Only about 55% of those students finished the class, and by our standards only a small handful should have been given the certificate because of the general lack of effort given to the training process and homework. They knew that showing up late would be tolerated, not doing the homework would also be shrugged off, and the financial investment was small enough that it didn't present a significant financial loss for the dog owners.

The clients who did the best job were the ones that needed the certificate so that they could keep their newly adopted dogs. The thought of losing their dogs was enough to motivate them to show up, do their homework and finish the program, while the other clients had no less of a need to do the work.

This simple fact is why I work with people who need dog training; I don't work with people who want dog training. It's very hard to get people to do the work after a long day at work if they don't need to. Surely some people do have classes that have much higher success rates, I'm not trying to suggest that it's not possible, but I do think that there is a strong correlation between how much a person invests financially and how much time and effort they invest into training their dog.

Understandably I often hear dog trainers suggest that it's not fair to charge a significant premium for your services because some will not be able to afford the price. I completely disagree with this sentiment. Unless the client is elderly and on a disability pension, there's a way for them to find some money to get the right training for their dog. Service dogs often cost $60,000 or more. Who has that kind of cash sitting around? That's why most service dogs are not purchased by the owners, they are purchased by the funds that are raised by local community groups. The person in need of a service dog has an extreme need for a dog to help them with mobility or other tasks and the person often will do anything to raise the money from others if they don't have the money themselves. When people have the desire, they find a way. If my dog needed a $3500 surgery next week and I didn't have the money, would I find the money? Yes. When I wanted to become a dog trainer, I wanted it so bad that I paid my mentor my entire life savings, slept on a dirty floor in a dog training facility a few times and ate rice and beans for six months. Why, because I wanted it badly enough.

This all seems very cold, I understand if you are feeling like I'm a money-hungry capitalist right now, but hear me out. I'm planning to train dogs for another 30+ years, and I'd rather work with highly motivated people over those 30 years instead of having to deal with the stress of working with less motivated clients. As suggested earlier in the book, I know people who have left the dog training industry because they worked with too many clients who didn't follow their advice and were stressful to deal with. Charging high prices is my insurance policy that grants me another 30 years of working with awesome people who put in the time.

I really like people and do give free advice and discounts depending on the situation. When someone comes in and is really struggling with the price, I hold to my price at the time. If they sign up, despite the financial difficulty, I secretly watch the clients for about 2-3 weeks to see how they are doing with the training. If they are doing the work and making a strong effort, I'll give them a portion of their money back as a surprise. Watching their mouths drop when I hand them an envelope full of cash is priceless. I then tell them that I had been watching them, and knew that it was difficult to find the money to pay for training. Typically these clients are students who are in college or university, disabled, or elderly.

In case you missed it, I don't let them know that I'm thinking about giving them a portion of the money back, because I want them to think that they are paying for the entire training program.

Many years ago I had a woman in her early twenties come in for an evaluation with her dog aggressive Saint Bernard. She saw the value in my services, and told me that she would have to get some money together and then she would call me and set up a time to start. Six months later she called me and wanted to start. She was proud to mention how she got a second job while going to university just to pay for the training. I signed her up; she did an incredible job, so I gave her an envelope full of cash after she had shown me that she was doing a great job. She was speechless.

If you want to check out my free video course for dogs trainers you can check it out here: www.tedsbooks.com/book-2-res

HOW TO PROPERLY BUILD TRUST
WITH CLIENTS

*M*ethods that dog trainers can use to build trust with clients:

• Being vulnerable with clients by telling them of your past mistakes and how you were able to overcome them
  • Do what you say you are going to do, every time
  • Pat your clients on the back when they do something well
  • Praise your client in front of others
  • Notice when your client makes an effort and praise them for that

So why is trust so important? When you build a strong base level of trust with your clients, they will refer you more clients, and forgive you when you make mistakes.

Have you ever forgiven someone quickly that you trust and respect, when they did something really stupid or insensitive? I sure have. We humans do it all of the time. We forgive our friends and family all of the time when they make a mistake because we don't want to hurt them by telling others of their stupid moments which would cause them harm. We humans tend to want to forgive those that we trust, and persecute those that we don't trust. Trust is one of the oldest forms of currency and likely goes back millions of years to our hunting and gathering days when being part of a trusted community was a matter of life and death. We want others to trust us, and we want to trust others because it makes us feel safe.

ALWAYS REBUKE clients behind closed doors and praise clients in front of others.

THIS LESSON IS one that all educators should learn before taking their first clients, and especially if they are going to run group classes. Praise people when others are watching and correct them only when you are alone.

In 2010 I was running one of my group classes for aggressive dogs at a local park and I did something really stupid. We had a small class that Saturday with only about 7 people. One client that I have not seen in several months came to the class with her young Border Collie. He was a handful and it was clear that the client had not been doing the work. Looking back on things, I should have had more empathy for her at the time as she was a mother with two busy young boys, this out of control dog and a husband that didn't want anything to do with training. Needless to say, she had a lot on her plate at the time.

Towards the end of the class, her dog jumped up and tried to bite her in the face when she asked her dog to lay down. Mortified, I grabbed her dogs leash and took him away. She was overwhelmed and she needed my support. Rather than helping her, I made her feel very small in front of the other clients. I suggested that she hadn't been to class in months and that they had not been doing any work with their dog and this was why their dog was acting out in class. She stood there silent, but her red eyes told a different story, if they could have spoken words, they would have said, "You just lost my trust you insensitive little jerk, and you'll never earn it back".

She held her tongue, but it was clear that internally she was hurting. We finished the class and everyone was acting awkward. When walking back to the car, I felt bad about how I had handled the situation, shifting the blame onto her, and so I apologized to her. She graciously accepted my apology, but I never saw her ever again. Suggesting that I blew it that day would be an understatement. I had made her feel small in front of other people, and I crossed a line that should never have been crossed. One of the other clients also stopped coming due to my insensitive blame-shifting moment, and as terrible as I felt for acting that way, I'm so grateful that I did act that way. Never again since that sunny Saturday afternoon in July of 2010 have I made another person feel so humiliated and misunderstood.

As you can see, you have everything to lose by shaming others, especially in a public setting, and this is always to be avoided. Don't look for the things that your client is doing incorrectly, look for the things that your client is doing correctly. Remember that pointing out your clients flaws will trigger in them a reflexive response that they are about to be kicked out of the tribe, and that will cause them to stop trusting you. Praising them and looking for things that they do well will have the opposite response and will help build and solidify trust.

DID you know that I help dog trainers with their businesses? If you are not yet a dog trainer and want an in-depth mentorship with me, go to: www.mangodogs.com/the-next-generation

IF YOU ALREADY HAVE A BUSINESS AND just want to come and work with me on your business for 10 days I have a program for that too! www.mangodogs.com/shadowted

HOW TO PROPERLY COMMUNICATE
WITH CLIENTS

The happiest dog trainers that I know are the best communicators. They know when to talk, they know when to listen, and they know how to voice their expectations.

WRITTEN homework is essential to your client's success

My mentor never gave his clients homework, and I remember when I was working with him, how often we would have clients come back each week with lackluster results. Vividly, I remember one man with his two dogs who was starting an off-leash program. The week earlier he had come in for his first lesson and he had a week to work on the foundation that the first lesson focused on. When starting the lesson, I asked him how the dogs were doing and how the week had gone, to which he had mixed emotions. "Well, the dogs were pretty good, but they kept chasing the horses all week" he noted. I remember instantly thinking to myself, wait, what? When did we tell you to let your dogs run off-leash around horses? It was in that moment that I realized that he had not been given proper, defined structure during our first lesson.

Soon after that lesson I started to write down very specific weekly homework for my clients to follow. I would print off the homework sheets in my office and be sure to have them ready to give to my client at the end of each lesson. Overnight I noticed a drastic decrease in how many questions I was getting by phone and email. Eureka! So simple, and so easy, and so effective.

If you work with basic obedience and puppy classes, it's very easy to make a step by step training syllabus that you can give to your clients after each lesson or class. For me, it's hard to have pre-printed homework sheets for my clients because all of my clients are in for different issues. To accommodate this, what I've done is create a basic text homework template on my computer, that I can copy and paste into my email program, and send as homework. This saves me dozens of hours each year because I don't have to type out instructions after each lesson. What used to take me 15 minutes per email homework, now takes about 2-3 minutes.

Another simple way to deliver homework that takes little to no time is to use video. At the end of the lesson I'll ask the client to pull out their cell phones. I'll get them to start recording a video, in which I'll tell them what the homework is, and then with their dog, I will demonstrate the homework right on the video. This method is simple, takes almost no time at all, and is very beneficial for your clients who have visual and audible learning styles. When they go home, they can playback the video as a reminder of the things you want them to do during the week.

HOW TO EVALUATE your clients learning style

All dog trainers know that each dog that we work with is an individual and they require a personalized approach, but often we forget to extend that same personalization over to the humans as well.

If you've been training dogs for any significant period of time, you may have watched on as your client trains one dog, with their other dog watching, waiting for their turn to take the stage. With 100% accuracy, I've noticed that the dog, who is watching, is also learning, and a process that took the first dog 30 minutes typically takes the second dog roughly half the time to learn. This same onlooker method is used by police dog trainers around the world to help build prey drive in their young police dog prospects. They put all of the puppies out in the yard, with leashes clipped to a wall of fence and allow the young dogs to watch the older dogs practice their bite work.

Knowing the major ways that humans and dogs learn is critical to becoming a great dog trainer, but few places in the world teach these basic concepts.

HUMANS CAN LEARN BY;

- Reading a book
- Hearing a description of how to accomplish a task
- Trying a task
- Doing a task
- Watching the task be done.
- Teaching the task

SOME HUMANS ARE VERY WELL SERVED by reading a book. I personally don't understand this position because I grow tired of books after just 5 minutes of reading. For some, their brains think in words, and books allow them the extra time to process what they are learning on their own time. Books are also great at how they present the information with consistency. The moment the document has been printed, it's unable to be altered which means that if the reader goes back to the document more than one time, no information will have changed.

Audible instruction is another way that humans are able to take direction and learn. I prefer audible instruction over the written word. When we hear something, I catch subtle things like tone that we are not able to pick up with the written word. Hearing instruction is also a great format because the medium can be consumed while the student is jogging, driving, or cooking dinner. It's impossible to read a book and go for a jog at the same time and this is the major reason why podcasts and audiobooks are gaining such popularity.

Allowing our clients the opportunity to learn by trying is a method that should only be used by an exceptional professional educator who is flawless at noticing the clients who will be benefited by this style of learning. The reason that I minimize this style of learning is because all of my clients have struggled far too much with their dogs already and they need as many quick wins as I can produce as a way to build their confidence.

There is some amazing scientific data on this topic that suggests we humans should have a lot of agency and freedom over what we are learning because as humans we have highly developed cognitive systems that desire to learn by natural discovery and trial and error. In my case, my clients don't want to figure it out; they want to pay me to shorten that learning curve exponentially. If the client has already tried a task and failed, like going for a walk and having their dog take off and attack another dog, more freedom will only alienate my clients and put them on the spot. They want me to hold their hand figuratively and sometimes literally.

At some point you will have to hand over the leash and let them figure things out, but this should be done when the client has been educated on the topic with many or all of the other methods available, to ensure that your clients have the tools to do a great job. Our job is to maximize the likelihood that our clients figure it out, and that's done best when we fully equip them by telling them how to do it, showing them how to do it, and allowing them to read instructions if needed. The main thing that you want to remember is to properly set up your client to do a great job before handing the leash over to them.

It's my experience that most dog owners are best served by visually watching the dog training process before trying to emulate the trainer. If you take video of previous lessons that you've taught, then upload them onto YouTube, you can email the video links to your new clients to watch before they start training. If you don't want people to be able to access the video unless you give them access, it's as simple as making the video an unlisted video when you upload to YouTube. Unlisted links will not be shown to the average viewer if you already have a YouTube channel, and the video will not be shared by popping up in a video feed if someone is searching for a related topic. Unless someone has the link to the video they cannot watch the video. There are three ways that I like to use video to teach my clients;

- Client watching a video of the trainer, training another person's dog
- Client watching a video of the trainer, training the clients dog
- Client watching a video of themselves training their own dog

EACH OF THESE video formats is good to use in teaching your clients, but you should know that the best is a blend of all three if possible. The way that I can achieve this for my clients is to send them videos of myself training dogs before we start training so that they have some context before we start to train. Then during the first lesson, have the client use their Smartphone camera to video record myself (the trainer) giving verbal homework instructions, followed by video of myself training their dog. Then I have the client hand me the phone and I record the client training their own dog as a reference.

If you are a professional dog trainer, you would already know how much you've learned when teaching clients to handle their dogs more effectively. Teaching is one of the best ways to learn because we must simplify the exercise and break it down into small little bit-sized piece that our clients can consume and mimic. While it might seem coun-terintuitive to get a client to teach something that they have just learned, it's a great way to help your client solidify what they are learning. It's important to educate the client to the point where they are proficient in the technique before getting them to teach someone else, but it's not essential for them to have the exercise perfectly mastered. You can integrate this teaching technique by teaching the client to do it first, and then have them teach you. Another option for families or clients with spouses is to get them to teach their spouse. Be sure to ask them to break each step down to help their spouse. When they give you or their spouse a play-by-play as they teach, the information will be more fully processed for both the student and teacher, and who knows, you might even learn something!

There are a few simple methods to help you notice which learning styles are resonating with your clients. In general I like to use a combination of these methods when I start training with a new client.

Follow *the engagement*

I'll take special notice when I see the client responding positively to a specific style of learning. When teaching theory, I watch to see if it's resonating with the client. If the client is engaged and asking questions, I will take more time on the theory part of the lesson. If I notice the opposite to be true I'll drop the theory and go directly into showing them how the training works to stimulate their visual senses.

Learning *about your clients*

Asking your clients simple questions about what they do for a living can often give you great insight into their learning style. I've had dozens of auto mechanics as clients over the years and I've yet to meet one that cared about learning theory on a whiteboard, but their eyes light up when you ask them if they want to grab the leash and give it a try. They tend to be very tactile and like practical learning. Psychologists are the exact opposite. They need hours to just talk through the process so that they feel like they have a handle on what they will be doing. The why must come before the how. A mechanic works with their hands for a living, and a psychologist talks and thinks for a living, so is it any wonder why the mechanic likes to grab the leash and the psychologist needs to talk for hours before getting started? Ask your clients about their hobbies and their careers, It might give you some insight that you can use to determine which learning style to start with.

Asking *your clients*

Writing down a small list detailing the different styles of learning and presenting it to your clients before you start training is a wonderful way to get valuable insight into the inner workings of your clients. Having a quick chat, or creating a quick 5 minute survey online will save you plenty of time during the training process because you can avoid wasting time trying to teach your clients in ways that will not move the needle. To gain this insight, simply lay out the basic learning styles for the client and ask them to rank each style with a rating of 1-10. Simply take the highest rated learning styles and focus on those styles. You can ask them simple questions like these;

- When learning about a new topic, do you prefer to read a book, listen to an audiobook, or watch a video?
- When learning a new skill, do you prefer to watch others practice, or dig right in and try things on your own?
- Would you consider yourself a confident person or more reserved?
- If your instructor were to call you to the front of the class to show others how to do an exercise, would you be mortified by the suggestion, be indifferent, or would you enjoy the limelight?

IF YOU WANT to check out my free video course for dogs trainers you can check it out here: www.tedsbooks.com/book-2-res

FIVE THINGS THAT COMPLETELY CHANGED MY BUSINESS FOR THE BETTER

1. Never invest more into your clients' success than they do

Few things in life are more aggravating than trying to convince a spouse, friend or family member that they need to change when they have no desire to change. As a dog trainer, you'll fall in love with dogs that are owned by people who also love their dogs, but might not be as committed to training as they need to be to make a lasting change in their dog's life. We've all done this, so don't beat yourself up if you have too. A dog owner calls, asking for help and all things look normal until you start to see signs that are troublesome. They show up late, they have plenty of excuses, and their dogs' bad behaviours are being exacerbated by the fact that they have a young, high energy dog and they only walk him two times a week.

When you question further, more excuses are brought to the surface. These clients always have an excuse for everything. "It's been a cold winter" the owner of a husky tells me as I try not to scream. Like you, I feel for this dog, so I try and give the owner some easy things to do that will make everyone's life easier. Often in cases like this I suggest that we train their dog to walk on a treadmill so that they don't have to go out as often in the cold, and the suggestion is met with an excuse. "We don't have room for a treadmill in our house" or "We don't have money for a treadmill". The issue is not with the lack of funds, you can buy a treadmill on craigslist for under $100. The issue is not with space, you can buy a fold up treadmill for under $200. The issue is that the clients want their dog to change without them having to do anything.

I really feel for dogs that are owned by selfish people like this, I really do. A small part of me cries inside when I meet a dog like this because I know that the dog is going to suffer a boring life because of their owner's selfishness. Suggesting that these owners should consider rehoming their dog is always met with more selfishness. "The kids would be crushed" is the most common response, or "Our dog would never be able to forget us, he would be crushed and never recover". Sorry to break it to you, but your dog would recover in a matter of minutes when they realize that there are humans in the world that are active and put the mental and physical needs of their dogs first. Allowing your kids to grapple with the realization that their parents are lazy is something that these owners want to avoid. They don't want to have to lie to their kids by telling them that they were not invested enough in the life and wellbeing of their dog to make the necessary sacrifices that are required to own a high energy dog. Keeping a dog that would be better served in another loving home is selfish, but it's impossible to get these owners to see that.

Present all of the training options, time requirements, financial obligations, and then put the owners in the driver seat. Every once in awhile you'll be surprised to see someone step up to the plate, and other times your see these owners cut you out of their dog's life because they don't like your advice. One thing that I do is give them an out. I always start with what they will need to change, the time requirements, etc, and then I'll throw in a way out. After giving them a detailed plan to get their dog where they need to be I will tell them "But you don't have to do any of this, it's going to be a lot of work and you'll need to make changes in your life, not everyone is cut out for having a well trained dog." Just that little option out is what many of these owners will take. While some owners will give up and finally come to the realization that they have bitten off more than they can chew, other will be greatly motivated by your cutting words. Nothing motivates me as much as someone telling me that I can't do something, and others are also wired that way.

It's not my job to try and convert the unconvertible. It doesn't matter how hard you try and convince me to be a communist, it's never going to happen. I'm never going to be converted, so why bother trying? You'll never convert a Hillary Clinton supporter to love Trump, or the other way around, so stop trying. Give the dog owner the roadmap to a better dog, then give them an out, and walk away and see if they actually follow up with you. It's not your job to help everyone, it's your job to help as many people and dogs as you can that are willing to make changes. Don't feel bad, even a master can't convince an uncommitted person to get to the gym everyday if they don't care about exercise or living a healthier life. Know your limits and don't focus on the dogs that you can't help, focus on the ones that you are helping. When I have a bad day and I find myself weighed down by worries brought on by problematic clients, I go to my website and read testimonials from hundreds of my past clients. The simple act of gratitude and focusing on what I have, instead of what I do not have, is an effective method of plucking me from the depths of negativity and pessimism.

2. TRUST YOUR GUT, and trust your dog, they know better than your emotions

Intuition, gut feeling, butterflies, whatever you call these feelings, It's my opinion that we should follow them when we are graced with their presence. There are millions of nerve endings in your gut that are activated when you have to contemplate a difficult decision or dangerous one, and this is your bodies alarm system. My gut feels off when I'm about to make a bad decision that I know will have long term consequences or when I'm avoiding doing something that I know is going to be socially uncomfortable. Have you ever met a dog and had the hair stand up on the back of your neck? This also seems to be another one of the alarm systems we humans can feel when in danger. I've had this happen a handful of times and all of those dogs turned out to be serious cases that would leave most trainers with nightmares for months.

Here are examples of two of the most intense dogs I have ever met, but did not present themselves as intense dogs the first time that I met them. Both dogs had a history of aggression, but were young and things were escalating quickly. When I met the dogs, instantly my hair stood up on the back of my neck and I felt something was horribly wrong. The dogs were not showing any outward signs that they were incredibly aggressive dogs, yet something inside of myself warned me. Just to be sure that my gut wasn't misdiagnosing the situation I brought in my Belgian Malinois BB who instantly confirmed my findings by shaking like a leaf just being in the same room as these dogs.

Trusting my gut is one thing, but having a trustworthy sidekick of a dog is essential in better defining if your gut feeling was right in the first place. These days I don't question my gut anymore because it's been right every single time it warned me. Using another dog for a second opinion is always a smart bet because they are the same species, but it's my view that many dogs are not able to get these same gut feelings. If you have a dog who is a good judge of character, never disregard your dog's sentiments if they throw up red flags. To avoid the wise counsel of a good dog is the pinnacle of arrogance and stupidity as a dog trainer.

3. PEOPLE WILL LIE to you

To suggest that I was gullible and naive at the start of my career would be an understatement. I struggled to come to terms with the realization that people could lie to someone just after asking for help, but I feel that I now have a more full view on why people lie to dog trainers today. There are two different types of lies;

• A LIE of commission is when a person tells you information that they know is not true
  • A lie of omission is when a person leaves out a piece of information that is pertinent to the conversation or fact

· · ·

It's very rare that a client will fabricate a lie; however, it's very common for people to leave out information that might be important to the trainer. The most critical piece in asking questions is to not ask open ended questions. Your questions or lack of questions could get you into trouble. If I ask a potential client if their dog has ever bitten anyone, I will get a plethora of answers depending on whom I ask. One person might be overly cautious and say yes, but I'm not sure what you mean by biting, do you mean play biting as well or just aggressive biting? Another might answer no despite knowing the answer is yes because they think that it will save them money if they convince the trainer that their dog is not dangerous. Some will say no, but when questioned further they reveal that their dog has bitten them several times. These people didn't think that such biting would count because their dog had a bone and they tried to take it from their dog.

The best way to navigate these treacherous waters of deception is to develop a keen sense of how to ask questions to get at the root of the issue. Asking a question like "Is your dog up to date on vaccinations?" is not a great question because it leaves far too much open to interpretation. Some people believe in the older model of vaccinating every year, while others believe in a three year vaccination schedule.

The most common lie that we dog trainers have to confront is the obvious lie. It's most often revealed when we ask our clients about things that they might feel guilty about. I really couldn't care less if a client allows their dog on the sofa, or bed, but I do ask the questions because I want to see how honest they are with me. It's common for clients to quickly turn away from you, avoid eye contact and stumble when giving their answer. The possibility of answers here is endless.

- Yes
  - No
  - Sometimes
  - Only on Saturday mornings
  - Only when we allow him up

- He gets on the bed when we go to work
- Only when he's scared during a thunderstorm
- He has his own bedroom and his own twin sized bed
- Yes, but not when friends come over

As you can see, an open ended question can insight many possible answers. Simply adding or subtracting a few words to a question can completely change the answer that you receive. Take these three questions for example.

- Do you let your dog on the bed?
    - Do you EVER let your dog on the bed?
    - Do you EVER allow your dog on the bed, and if so, do you feel guilty about that? If you feel guilty about that, why?

Asking a more defined question will get you closer to a complete and truthful answer.

Feel free to ask follow-up questions if you don't get a complete answer the first time around.

- Do you agree or disagree with allowing him on the bed?
    - Is this a point of tension in your relationship?
    - Do you like your dog sleeping in the bed with you, or do you feel guilty when you ask him to get off the bed?
    - What do you like about your dog sleeping on the bed? Does it make you feel safe or are you allowing it out of obligation?

The most important question that you can ask a potential client is "Has your dog EVER bitten anyone, for any reason?" Make sure to look at them in the eyes when you ask the question. If you get anything but a definitive NO, you need to ask follow-up questions to figure out what the client is not telling you.

Look at the owners in the eyes when you ask this question. If the client says no and then quickly looks away, it's very possible that the client has just lied to you or is hiding something. It's my experience that very few dog trainers ask this question because they are rushing. Don't rush when you are training dogs, even if the dog looks friendly. The next time that you take a dog's leash could be the difference between a great training lesson or the last lesson that you ever teach. The questions that you ask can mean the difference between life and limb for you, so don't hesitate to ask the tough questions and be sure that they are very defined.

4. YOU CAN'T SAVE *them all*

As a dog trainer I'm limited to helping only the dogs that are owned by humans who ask for help and are willing to invest time into their dogs. Not being able to save every dog is not just something that dog trainers have to deal with, but it's especially true in the dog rescue world. For many years I've helped out in dog rescue and I can tell you that you cannot save every dog. I wish this statement was not true, but it is. It's important to know your limitations. If you care as much about dogs as I do, it will be difficult for you to step back when you hear of a dog that is in need of training. Remind yourself that your training help will leave no lasting impact unless the dog that's being trained has ongoing support. My goal is not to save the world, it's to help the people and dogs that God puts in my path each day to the best of my ability without compromising my families mental health, safety, or financial security. Drawing a line in the sand can be difficult for many dog trainers because we get so invested in the dogs that come into our lives. I hope that this chapter helps you as you learn the difference between when you are helping and when you are hurting.

A few years ago I watched a movie called "Shotgun Preacher". Midway through the movie the main character, a preacher in Africa, was driving a large cargo truck filled with supplies to people in need when he drove past a large pit. As he neared the side of the pit he heard human screams. He stopped the truck and approached the pit on foot, stumbling upon a tragic sight. Hundreds of people were down in this pit and in need of help. Helping one of them out of the pit, he asked why they were all trapped. The man responded by saying there was a band of militia who had taken them hostage, thrown them into this pit with no food or water and warned them that they would be back soon to slaughter them all.

The preacher helped the vulnerable people out of the pit, unloaded the cargo from his truck and then made arguably one of the hardest decisions any human has ever had to make. Cramming people into every tiny spot inside and on top of his truck, he fit about 100 people into his cargo truck. He then had to decide if they would stay and fight without any weapons or if he would drive to the nearest camp, drop the people off and go back for the remaining people. The remaining people could not just walk or run away and hide because they were in the desert without anywhere to hide. In the end the driver saved the 100 people's lives and did not have time to save the remaining people without also being killed.

It's been about a decade since I watched that movie so I hope that the facts are accurate and to my recollection it's also a true story. This true story is a difficult one, but I think that we can draw from it a greater understanding that will allow us to process a very real and difficult part of our jobs. Some dogs cannot be saved because of serious neurological issues. Some dogs develop serious cases of aggression because they have an untreated brain tumor and they are not able to be saved. We have to come to terms with the fact that we are not Gods and Goddesses. Our ability with dogs is often something that attracts people who are unwilling or unable to help their own dog and these people might want to surrender their dog to us. While I feel grateful that people contact me to surrender their dogs instead of just dumping them on the street and driving away, I can't help every single dog that comes into my life. Most of these dogs have a lot of behavioural or aggressive issues, and some have long term health issues. The raw truth about the situation is that if I said yes to every person who wanted to surrender their dog to me, I would have a home with hundreds of dogs, I would be broke, my wife would have left me, and I would be extremely resentful.

One night I was praying and I felt like God was inspiring me to give more of my time, skills, and money to those in need. At that moment I heard the words "Give until it hurts you, but stop giving when it hurts others". Maybe this is good advice for us all. Giving is one of the most reliable ways to ensure that you live a fulfilled life. The issue is that giving can turn into something that's not benefitting anyone if it's not given a finish line.

A good finish line for dog trainers who work with rescue dogs might be that you will work with 1 or 2 fosters at a time, and then you leave one month off for resting and rejuvenation. The thing that we need to remind ourselves is that giving endlessly is not a sign of strength, it's a sign of weakness. Not being able to say no is not a good thing. When you get a call and the rescue wants you to take another dog but you know that your husband is ready to walk out of your marriage because you already have 7 dogs, your giving has now become a curse.

You can only do as much as you can do and that's it. It's not your responsibility to fix everyone's situation because you simply can't. Saying yes is easy, saying no is hard. Take care of your mental health, your family, your dogs, and do what you can for others with what is left of your time and resources. If you gave away 100% of your money to a local rescue, you would lose your home, have to live on the street with your dogs and not be able to help others. We always leave enough financial resources to pay the mortgage, but many trainers don't have a moment of time left at the end of the week to enjoy their life. Why is that? When the bank account is overdrawn, it's easy to know that you have a problem, but you can't overdraw on time, so we always feel that we have enough.

I have a friend who is an incredible person, he has 16 dogs at home. He's worked in rescue for many years and has a heart of gold. But when we've talked about his dogs in the past, he clearly resents most of them. He took them in because the rescue that he worked with made him feel bad when he would say no to another dog, and now 6 years later he is in a difficult situation. His lack of commitment to the word no, only took hold when they got to dog number 16. For some reason 16 was his breaking point. The point by which he told the rescue he would never help them again because he thought they had taken advantage of him. All of the dogs had significant issues which means that some of them can't be around other dogs. This means that some of his dogs are living in a dog crate for much of their lives. Surely he saved these dogs' lives, but they are not living an abundant life.

He's resentful because he can't travel anymore. Boarding 16 dogs at the same time would cost thousands of dollars a week, which he doesn't have. He's resentful because he feels bad for his first two dogs, Mika and Ottis. His dogs were his best friends and now they never get any alone time with their owner because he's too busy feeding and exercising the rest of the rescue dogs. Not a great life for my friend or the dogs if you ask me. He once told me something that really drove the point home. "I'm honestly just waiting for them to die so that I can get my life back". At some point, all good things become a bad thing when we allow too much of it in our lives. Take time to care about how your spouse, kids, and your dogs feel about the situation or you might just lose those who are closest to you.

5. ASSUME *that every dog is going to try and bite you*

One of the best parts of my job is that I have the ability to teach dog trainers around the world by way of my online coaching programs and my ten day dog trainer shadowing programs. When I'm mentoring other trainers, I always start by teaching them how to be careful around dogs. I repeatedly impress upon my students how important it is to set up systems and procedures in their businesses that help them minimize the likelihood of them being bitten. At first glance, most trainers brush off this information wanting to get to more advanced dog training concepts, but I persist because I know the importance of what I'm teaching them. What good are dog training skills if you are attacked by a dog and end up needing to change careers?

It's my view that the vast majority of dog trainers do not focus nearly enough on safety and sometimes that lack of focus can come back to bite them when they least expect it. This advice is as important for agility trainers as it is for trainers who work with dangerous dogs. In many ways I think that it's safer to work with aggressive dogs because it's easier to take things seriously when you know that a dog has a bite history. You've heard it said by most dog trainers that it's the small dogs that you have to watch out for, and while that's true, I would suggest that it's all dogs that you need to watch out for. If you train hundreds of dogs a year, it's only a matter of time before you are bitten, but you can greatly decrease those odds if you are cautious and vigilant with each and every client.

I consider myself lucky that I've been working with aggressive dogs everyday for over a decade and have only been bitten once, but in reality, a large reason why I only have one scar on my hand is because I'm systematic about safety. Almost every day I hear trainers say that if you are going to work with dogs, you need to be ready to be bitten because it's going to happen. That's true, but it's often suggested with the intention that these incidents will be frequent and that there is nothing that you can do about it because it's inevitable. I disagree with both of these inferred statements. If you are being bitten regularly, you are doing something terribly wrong.

If it's common for you to be bitten as a dog trainer, please don't take offense to these statements because they are not meant to be malicious. I've even met some trainers who wore their scars like medals of honour, showing them off to clients, friends, and family in an effort to prove as if dog bites are to be seen as a right of passage. It's always been male trainers who have the bravado to boast about dog bites, but I don't see the same with female trainers. Female trainers don't seem to have this same fascination with proving themselves through war wounds. Regardless of your gender, nothing about being bitten should be seen as a positive unless it's being highlighted in an effort to teach others how to avoid being bitten. I often tell other trainers about the time I was bitten on the hand, but not to boast, rather to illustrate why it's so important to learn from your mistakes. Being bitten is not a sign of significance, it's a sign of weakness. Boasting about being bitten is like bragging about how many car accidents you've been in, in an effort to convince people that you're a good driver.

If you are a basic obedience trainer or work with problematic dogs, you should assume that every dog is going to try and bite you every single time you are around dogs, even if you are not holding the leash. Assuming each dog will try and bite you will dramatically decrease your trips to the emergency room. Every time I'm near a client's dog, or around other people's dogs, my guard is up. I'm assuming that the dog is going to try and bite me, even when I'm at the park and there are dogs running around. To illustrate why this is important to assume, I'll use a story to explain.

In the early part of my career, I was starting with a new dog, a German shepherd named Indi. Indi was by all measures a good dog, and his owners asked me to help them work on his recall and a few behavioural issues. At the midway point of our first lesson, I went to put a collar and long leash on Indi when I was almost bitten. Indi lunged at me when I walked towards him with the collar and leash and was just inches from biting me. Lucky for me, the owner was still holding his leash so I narrowly escaped a potentially bad bite. Indi did not growl at me before he lunged, so the whole thing happened very quickly. Now I know that I reinforced his lunging behaviour at that moment, but I was surprised and obviously wanted to avoid being bitten.

I had asked the client during our first meeting (the evaluation) if Indi had ever bitten anyone to which she said no, which is why this incident seemed to be out of character. Receiving that no from her had caused me to assume he would be fine. Assumption can lead to dog bites. After collecting my thoughts I asked the client the same question again and she told me that he did always tries to bite his veterinarian. She wondered if Indi thought that I was a veterinarian. Given the fact that I was not wearing a white jacket, and we were in a large open space, that didn't seem probable, however, I could not understand why this client had not thought it fitting to tell me about how he acts at the vet.

. . .

THIS SITUATION HAPPENED EARLY in my career and it completely changed the way that I approach my business and safety. Here are a few lessons from my time working with Indi.

• Don't assume that the client is telling you the truth, or even a half a truth

• Always ask the client how the dog behaves at the vet

• Have the client put leashes and collars on the dog so that you don't put yourself in a potentially compromising situation

• Look at the client in the eyes when you ask them if their dog has ever acted aggressively towards any people, for any reason

• Assume that each dog is going to try and bite you, even if the owner suggests that their dog is safe

THESE SIMPLE TIPS have saved me over the years from countless potential bites, and they can save you too. Just months before Indi lunged at me I was bitten by only one dog, even to this day. I had come to trust that dog and was not prepared when he bit me because I thought he would be fine, because of all the other times he was fine with me approaching him. While that bite hurt a lot, it also taught me a lot. I didn't blame the dog, I blamed myself. That bite could have been prevented if I had been more diligent about preparing for a worst-case scenario. Keep safe, you owe it to yourself, your career, future clients, family, and friends.

DID you know that I help dog trainers with their businesses? If you are not yet a dog trainer and want an in-depth mentorship with me, go to: www.mangodogs.com/the-next-generation

IF YOU ALREADY HAVE A BUSINESS AND just want to come and work with me on your business for 10 days I have a program for that too! www.mangodogs.com/shadowted

HOW TO EVALUATE IF YOUR POTENTIAL CLIENT IS READY TO CHANGE

*T*his next chapter might be the most important chapter in this book because it will help you find your way to the Promised Land of great clients. Knowing when people are ready to change is vital, but a very difficult skill to learn. When a client contacts you and asks for help, most trainers assume that the person is willing to invest time, money and to make some life changes. In reality, this does not at all mean that they are ready to change; in fact, all that it means is that they have taken some quick steps to seek help. As discussed earlier in this book, you can't buy a six-pack, and it's essential to find clients that are willing to put in the time to get that six-pack of a dog.

In human psychology, there is a behavioural change model that is widely used to explain human behavioral changes. Published in 1983, Prochaska & DiClemente's model (1983) is a simple way for anyone to evaluate if a potential client is ready to change.

STAGE 1 - PRE-CONTEMPLATION
No interest in changing behavior.

. . .

STAGE 2 - CONTEMPLATION

The person is aware of a problem but has made no commitment to change thus far.

STAGE 3 - PREPARATION

The person intends on taking action to correct the problem.

STAGE 4 - ACTION

The person is in active modification of behavior.

STAGE 5 - MAINTENANCE

Sustained change occurs and new behaviors start to replace the old ones.

STAGE 6 - RELAPSE

The person falls back into old patterns.

STAGE 7 - UPWARD spiral

Each failure will reset the cycle; however, the person will be better equipped on the next attempt.

TO SIMPLIFY this model for dog trainers, I've decided to use the cycle of change as a base for a new model just for you. The cycle of change for dog trainers.

STAGE 1 - THINKING about things

My dog is fine, he's just spirited.

· · ·

STAGE 2 - We might need some help soon

The owner's back is sore from the leash pulling, but the pain point is not yet strong enough to have to address the root cause.

STAGE 3 - SENDING emails and making phone calls

The owner is looking for help by asking friends if they know anyone who can help, they look at a few websites, make a few calls and send a few emails. The intention is to aggregate data until they need to call someone, that time will come soon.

STAGE 4 - The wheels are in motion

The owner is now reading a book, watching a video, or working with a trainer. They have taken the leap and made a time/financial commitment to train their dog.

STAGE 5 - MAINTENANCE

The client is seeing results and they now have more tools and ideas to keep on the right path.

STAGE 6 - STOPPED doing the work

The person falls back into old patterns. They have not yet learned that if they stop putting in the time, the results will go away.

STAGE 8 - SEEKING additional support

The clients reach back out to their training or resource. They learn that it's common for clients to stop doing the work, and so they go back to doing the work and for that, they once again receive the results they once had.

STAGE 7 - Back again at the starting point

Each relapse in the dog's behaviour will result in the client starting the cycle once again. Going back to what they know works, but each time, adding a new idea or tool to get to the next level.

It's not a given that just because someone is thinking they need a dog trainer, that they will call a dog trainer. Let the client decide when they are ready to take the first steps, and know that first steps are often just that. It's not a given that someone thinking they need a dog trainer will take time out of their schedule or money out of their bank account to train their dog. Just because someone emails you asking for help, that does not mean that they will actually sign up for training or do the work.

Often times when a client starts training they choose the cheapest dog training classes with the hopes that they can get away with a quick generic fix. This is incredibly common and often leads to the client progressively purchasing more and more training until the problem is finally solved. This is why I refuse to hold inexpensive classes for people whose dogs have behavioural problems. The classes are overwhelming for them and their dog, and they end up feeling like a failure. My weekly classes are only open to the owners of rescue dogs that I have worked with, and for my clients who have done extensively private training with me already.

It should not be assumed that the client will sign up even if they have a significant issue with their dog. Timing is essential, if you push for a sale, you might find yourself spending time with a human that is not ready to change.

3 months ago I got a call from a man named James. He had a young rescue dog named Odin. He sounded very concerned about his dog's behaviour, and it was clearly a big issue in his life. Over a 20 minute conversation, he told me Odin's life story and how his wife was ready to take him back to the shelter because of his leash reactivity. Both of them were struggling to walk him without feeling like complete failures. After allowing him to vent for some time, I told him how much time it would take and the cost. It was clear that the cost was an issue, without him saying that it was. He told me that he would call me back

76

and thanked me for my time. One month later, his wife called me. Another 20-minute conversation and a suggestion that she would call me back. Two more months went by and then James called back. They were ready, they wanted to start ASAP. They did start right away and have been great clients and they are thrilled with Odin's progression.

So why did I leave the clients to anguish for three months before we started to train Odin? They needed those months to reach rock bottom. It was some dirty looks from neighbours and rude comments that finally pushed them to sign up. Don't rush the process; let it run its course.

Long phone calls and novel like email tend to be a big waste of time for dog trainers, at least in the short term. In Odin's case, it just took a few more months for his owners to pull the trigger and get started, but for many dog owners, they never pull the trigger. Over the years, I've noticed a trend in my email inbox. The longer the email, the less likely people are to sign up. If there is a photo enclosed, the odd's decrease even more. This is not just a made-up theory, I've investigated further with many other trainers, and 100% of them have noticed the same trend.

THE FOLLOWING IS an email I received recently, the writer of the email never called me to take me up on a free evaluation.

BELLA HAS STARTED ATTACKING TACO. *This has happened four times now and this has traumatized and devastated me. I have had dogs all my life and never had to rehome, and don't want to, but I can't live like this. I talked to -- ---------- who used to train police dogs for the RCMP. He told me he believes that I am the problem in that Bella sees me as hers and herself as mine and is possessive of me and does not want to share me. Why is it Taco that she attacks and not Jonnie? This happened for the first time I believe in August of this year at 0420 one morning. I was sleeping and Taco and Bella were both on the bed with me which was the way it has always been and up to this point they used to lie together, lick each other's ears, etc. and fall asleep often with legs around each other or one with their head resting on the other. I don't know what started it, but all of a sudden there is a dog fight going on and I was trying to get to the light switch and in breaking them up I got bit in the process but I truly believe they did not mean to, I just got in the way as I was trying to separate them. The next time was approximately Sept. 1 or 2 and it was in the daytime and they both had come in my room and there was nothing that he did that I could see and she was on him and it was terrifying. I went to get up to get out of the way and to get something to try to separate them again and I fell and they landed on top of my legs and again I got bit and I don't even know by which dog, and that time I required stitches and they did more damage to each other in terms of bites. I consulted my vet, Dr. - ------------- at -------------- Animal Hospital in ----------- at that time and he put Bella on clomipramine 50mg twice a day. Clomipramine is a people antidepressant that is supposed to work as an anti-anxiety and seda- tive on dogs. He was hoping just to give her a reset and get her through what- ever was going on with her. In the meantime and for approximately two weeks I kept them totally separated, crating one when the other was out and vice versa. All along Jonnie was and is fine with either dog. Everything had been going well and they were playing together fine since then and no further issues until about two weeks ago and again she attacked him and I blame myself because I had let my guard down a bit and it happened when they both came in my bedroom. The fourth time it happened was two days ago and each time there does not seem to be anything that Taco does, but then I'm not a dog and I don't know if he "said" something to her but in all honesty, I really don't think so, I really don't. Taco is a sweet, sweet boy and has had no issues at all with Jonnie. Taco and Bella are fixed, Jonnie is intact as I am a believer that with the giant breeds you need to let the growth plates complete before neuter- ing, he will be done at age two. Jonnie is a sweet boy and not a fighter at all. And I hesitate to say it because I can't stand the reaction I get from people when I say how sweet Bella is, it's like "Oh ya, she sounds some sweet." And I will still say it, she is so loving and she had always gotten along fine with both my dogs and she's totally sweet to her people, you couldn't find a more loving dog. Bella is 88 lbs of pure muscle, Taco is 114 lbs and Jonnie is 160 lbs, all big dogs. I never would have picked a Cane Corso for myself, I love the English mastiff breed and my son gave her to me when I had lost three dogs in a six month period and struggled with the loss of the last one, an English mastiff who died from cancer after he had survived atrial fibrillation for several years with frequent trips to pei under the care of Cardiology and was doing fantastic and then cancer hit. Patrick couldn't find an EM puppy but instead found Bella and got her for me. And of course it took a bit but I did fall in love with her and she was fantastic with Patrick's Newf, Winston, who was living with me at the time. When he was going to be leaving the end of the summer I said how lonely she would be without him and we rescued Taco, his family were giving him up to the SPCA as they were moving and couldn't take him, I will never understand that as he has been the most amazing dog from the get-go and my son had taken Bella with them to pick him up to see if they were compatible and they loved each other from the start. Then I found a breeder in --------- and added ---------- as I just couldn't be without an English mastiff, that is my breed, they are a heartbreak breed as they don't usually last as long being a giant breed but their personality is in my eyes just so amazing and I can't see me as not always having one. Anyway, I love my dogs and really don't want to rehome Bella, it will kill me and I fear that someone else may abuse her and I can't stand the thought of that. One of the girl's at Dr. -------------- suggested you to me and I am reaching out for your help so that I at least give it every possible chance. Thank you*

I GET emails and phone calls like this all of the time. Every time I read these emails I feel bad for the writer and I want to reach out and help, but I have to remind myself that the writer might be very early in the cycle of change and not ready to take steps to get help. There is no one else in my area that will work with 100lb + dogs that are fighting in the same home, so I know that she didn't get help from another trainer. I can only hypothesize, but the writer is either still living in a very unsafe situation, has euthanized one or both of her dogs, or rehomed one or both of her dogs. She did not take the initiative to return my email or call. If we take a moment to dive into the email, the writer takes no time to say hello. She assumes that I know multiple people that she names, who I do not know, she doesn't ask me for help, she ends her email saying that she's contacting me because she promised her Vet that she would. I hope for the sake of the writer and her dogs that all is well in her home. Her email was not asking for help, it was a rant.

BELOW IS another recent email that I received. The owner did not contact me for help after her initial email.

HI TED,

I'M WRITING to inquire about training services.

WE HAVE a 6-year-old female Cane Corso. She was originally our dog, and we had to move to Montreal for work and she went to live with my in-laws. When we had her, we trained her about 2 hours a day and gave her the exercise required for her breed, All of which stopped when she moved in with the in-laws.

MY FATHER in law recently passed and we are moving our mother in law in with us. Along with Blue (the dog). There are some red flags that make me extremely nervous, and because of how large she is, it makes those worries so much bigger.

SOME CONCERNS I HAVE ARE:
    -She pulls terribly and is animal aggressive while on leash. (She has bitten crows right out of bushes before) and she does not like tiny breeds of dogs/cats.
    -She is a guard dog by nature, which is absolutely fine. But when anyone walks by the house or the mail comes she will bark until they have left and does not stop when told.
    -My son is 8 and has super high functioning Aspergers. She will not allow him to pet her because as he goes to pet her, his other hand is wiggling around

80

in the corner of her eye and freaks her out causing her to growl/bear teeth at
him. As we will be moving in together this is my huge concern.

SHE'S *a good dog who wants structure, just has been treated like a human for*
the last 4 years. I have only ever trained puppies, and have not had to correct
negative behaviour in a full-grown dog. So I'm feeling at a loss. Any infor-
mation on pricing and services would be greatly appreciated.

THANK YOU,

KNOW that you can't force people to actually get help. The most
desperate emails pleading for help are often not followed upon. If you
want to determine if the potential client is ready to change, the best
thing that you can do is to give them something that they need to do.
As them to call you and book a time to meet and talk about training
options, and even then many of these owners are not ready to sign up.
You can also ask them to send over Vet records for their dog or to fill
out some forms pertaining to their dog. Don't get invested until they
get invested. Make them take action before you take action.

IF YOU WANT to check out my free video course for dogs trainers you
can check it out here: www.tedsbooks.com/book-2-res

HOW TO RESOLVE CONFLICT WITH CLIENTS

*M*any of the chapters in his book were specifically devoted to weeding out unmotivated clients before they become a headache, but despite that advice, there will be moments you find yourself having to deal with conflict with clients. For me it's incredibly rare that I deal with conflict, I might have a glimpse of conflict about once a year, but nonetheless, it still happens. Your client evaluation process will never be 100%, but I want to emphasize that if you pick your clients properly and set proper boundaries before training, these issues should greet you as often as the common flu.

In dealing with conflict, there are 8 conflicts I noticed most often over the years;

1. CONFLICTS over being late
   2. Conflicts over scheduling
   3. Conflicts over cancellations
   4. Conflicts over training results
   5. Conflicts over tools and techniques
   6. Conflicts over not having a concrete game plan
   7. Conflicts over payment

8. Conflicts over refunds

When you are driving to a client's home, you should be a few minutes early. Sit in their driveway and wait until the exact minute, then go knock on the door. There is no excuse for being late, ever. Being late is disrespectful, and tells others that you don't manage your time well. If there is traffic that causes you to be late, you should have left your home earlier. Unless your car breaks down and has to be towed away, you don't have an excuse. If you are late often, you need to book fewer clients in a given day so that you have more time to drive to your client's home and give a buffer time in case of traffic or a much-needed bathroom break. If you are late, own up to it, promise to never do it again and do just that.

If you have a facility and your clients come to your location to meet you, you'll need to tell your clients over the phone and email that you expect them to be on time or a few minutes early. When people come for an evaluation, it's our first time meeting and I want to start things off on the right foot. If you tell potential clients how important it is to you that they are on time or early, you will naturally get fewer people arriving late. If they are late, you should not shrug it off, you should address the fact that they are late politely. If you don't, these clients will be much more likely to be late in the future when you start training. Not only are potential clients reminded to be early or on time for lessons before we meet, but the same message is written on my training program quote sheet that every potential client receives at the end of our meeting.

It's astounding how effective these little reminders are. Late clients are made when we don't communicate our expectations at the beginning of the relationship. Remember that people will treat you the way that you allow them to treat you, even good people cannot make your time a priority unless you make it known that your time is valuable.

WE TEACH people how to treat us.

IF YOU DON'T HAVE the confidence to tell potential clients not to be late and include it in your company's sales information because you think it's going to cost you potential sales, I have good news for you. Including this information will increase the number of sales that you get. People, who are looking for a dog trainer, are not seeking a doormat, they want someone who is confident, and being upfront with people, while it will seem extremely counterintuitive in the beginning is actually a great sales tactic and will cut down drastically on your headaches.

CONFLICTS OVER SCHEDULING

Dog trainers are notorious for not being great at time management. Many times we overbook our days in an effort to get in more clients which makes us more money. This overbooking is usually rooted in the fear of not being confident enough to raise our prices but can also be driven by our need to please everyone. If you are busy, and you are a people pleaser, you might find yourself saying yes to too many clients in an effort to please everyone that asks for your help. When you are run ragged, you are not doing anyone a favor. You are putting yourself in a very dangerous position because your ability to stay safe and be at your best is only possible if you are well-rested, well-hydrated and in good mental health. Ensuring that you don't have scheduling conflicts is simple, just communicate with your clients from the beginning which days and times you are available for lessons. If your schedule does not align with their schedule don't take them as a client. If you are too booked up and feeling overwhelmed, start referring potential clients to other local trainers who would have more time to take on new clients.

CONFLICTS OVER CANCELLATIONS

These conflicts are likely the most common and are completely avoidable. Again, proper communication on this topic is essential to limiting or eliminating conflict over cancellations. In over a decade of working with clients and dogs full time I don't think I ever canceled one lesson, I even showed up when I was sick. You should have a similar mindset if you expect your clients to show up for their lessons. For trainers who run group classes, you need to tell people multiple times how your classes work. Tell them over the phone, on your website, and over email. Don't assume that they have been to your website and seen your term and policies about cancellations and refunds.

If you do mainly private training lessons, always tell your clients before they sign up that if they need to cancel, there is a process for that. Be sure to educate your clients on your policy before signing them up. Here's what I suggest as a cancellation policy;

SO HERE'S THE DEAL, your time is valuable and my time is too. I won't cancel last minute on you if you promise not to do the same to me. If you need to cancel because of an emergency you can do that. Once. If you have to, please give me 36 hours if possible so that I can book a client that I like better in your spot :) Unless you are car jacked on the way home from work by a man in a clown suit, I'll expect to see you at our appointed sessions. P.s. If you see someone approaching your car in a clown suit, step on the gas!

THIS CHEEKY LITTLE paragraph can save you countless hours of frustration, feel free to use my policy or come up with your own little kick in the pants policy.

Conflicts over training results

If a client is not told what they can expect and roughly how many hours it will take them to achieve these results, they can easily get irritated, and rightfully so. Many years ago I went to a trainer with my first dog Phoenix. The shelter that I adopted him from had referred me to this trainer and had made him seem like a miracle worker. After he took my money and didn't teach me anything even remotely practical, I felt like someone had taken advantage of me. Luckily for me, he is the reason I'm a dog trainer today. His lack of self-awareness and unwillingness to help me and my dog were the reasons I became a dog trainer in the first place. Don't be a trainer who teaches stupid, useless things to people who are struggling with their dog.

If you do basic obedience classes, don't let out of control dogs into your class until they are ready. The people will be overwhelmed, the dog will make a scene, you will be stressed, and the people will go home feeling like losers. Every single day I have dog owners come in, asking for help, real help; the help that will get to the root of the issue in a reasonable amount of time. If you can't provide that service, don't take money from people with problematic dogs.

Conflicts over tools *and techniques*

Because I'm a balanced dog trainer, I use both positive and negative motivation in training, and at times this can be a conflict for potential clients. Every once in awhile I'll have someone call me and tell me how their Vet referred them to me because I'm "the best guy to call if you have an aggressive dog". Naturally, the conversation steers to talking about methodology and tools. 95% of these conversations go well and lead to meeting in person, but about 5% of the time the client is completely unwilling to use any type of negative motivation in training. To that I say "Ok great, so here are a few phone numbers of people you can call that will best fit your training methodology."

I DON'T TRY and convince someone that the way I would train their dog is the right way unless they are willing to listen and be open. I could be inauthentic and try to train them in methods that I don't believe will fully get to the root of the problem, but that's not going to help anyone. If you are a force-free trainer, it's assumed that you would do the same right? We just need to be honest with people so that they know what they will be doing, and how long it will take to get good, consistent results.

86

. . .

CONFLICTS over not having a concrete game plan

Before a potential client signs up to your dog training service you should answer these questions for them;

- HOW MUCH THE training will cost them
  - What they will be learning
  - Why they will be learning it
  - How long it will take to get results
  - How long they will need to keep up with the training

ANSWERING these questions will set an appropriate foundation with your clients so that they know what to expect. If my first trainer had properly answered these questions for me, I would have never signed up to his training program because I would have seen it to be a huge waste of time and money.

If the client signs up to your training, you'll want to give them weekly homework to follow. Believe it or not, most dog trainers don't give their clients detailed homework. If you identify with this behaviour, you'll be pleased to know that you can dramatically decrease the number of phone calls and emails that you get from clients who need clarification.

CONFLICTS OVER PAYMENT

If you've ever had to press a client to pay you, or not pay you at all, you'll want to make some changes to the way that you do business. Instead of just assuming that your clients are going to pay you on time, you really should have some systems in place to ensure that you don't have payment drama in your business.

Some trainers rely on their clients to pay them each time that they meet for a lesson. Personally I much prefer that my clients pay me before the training starts whenever possible so that we can get that out of the way. Allowing clients the opportunity to pay during each session creates unnecessary paperwork and will take away from your training time. I have my clients pay either 100% on the first lesson, or 50% during the first lesson and 50% about one month later when we have made significant improvements to their dogs' behaviour. Because I also provide unlimited group classes for my clients, they have to make their final payment before they transition into the classes, which helps increase the likelihood of the clients making both payments. If my clients choose to pay with the 50/50 method, they must also sign a payment contract and leave a credit card on file giving me the authorization to run the final payment on a specified date.

Many trainers have their clients pay 100% of the fee the day they book the first lesson. I can fully understand why they might do this, but I would caution newer trainers from doing this because you might lose some potentially good clients who might go to another trainer that has payment options. Another option is to have the client make a non-refundable payment to secure their space in your schedule. If they cancel, you will keep the payment and will re-book their space with another client.

Conflicts over refunds

All of my clients are told in person during the evaluation, and on their evaluation quote sheet, that I do not provide any refunds or exchanges of any kind and of course my website also serves this purpose. My clients fully understand the gravity of what they are getting into before they give me any money or commit to training. In fact I actually tell my clients that the moment that they give me money, it's not money that they will ever get back, and so they should seriously contemplate what they are about to get into. The clients are also reminded of this in their liability/payment contract. Because of my upfront attitude about these issues, I have only been asked for a refund once, and I have only given a refund one time. Considering that I have over 1250 clients, that number speaks for itself.

Earlier in this book I told the story of a woman with a greyhound who was human and dog aggressive. She was given a full refund, not because she asked for one but because I wanted her out of my life as soon as I possibly could. If you remember the story, she lied to me multiple times and those lies put myself and my dogs in harm's way. I made the decision to give her the refund not because I was obligated to give her one and not because she asked. I gave her the refund because she was a person that I could no longer trust, and for me to give her a full refund was a great investment in my mental health. Given her past lies, I determined that she could be the type of person who might make up more lies and spread them around the internet which could cost me a lot of clients in the future.

Never underestimate how much damage a person can do to your business when they feel rejected. The squeaky wheel gets the grease, so be careful who you mess with. One seriously angry client could cost your business hundreds of thousands of dollars in lost sales if they are active on the internet.

For many trainers that I've talked to, they don't like to provide refunds because of a moral standard that most trainers feel bothered by. They feel that because they invested time with a client that they should be compensated for that time regardless of the outcome of the relationship. I would never judge a trainer for having that line of thinking. I've personally thought a lot about this topic and have come to the conclusion that it's just not worth the time or drama to try and fight someone who wants a refund.

Luckily for myself, I have only had one refund request, so it's not a mental battle that I need to have often. If you properly communicate with clients before training, you will dramatically decrease the number of refund requests.

The one and only time that I was asked for a refund happened less than one year ago. I assumed that the client was going to be challenging because she was open with me that she had been struggling with serious depression. While most trainers run from these clients like they have the plague, I embrace them because I too have struggled with anxiety and depression in the past so I feel that in some ways I'm uniquely qualified to work with such clients. This client was amazing at the start. She paid for her training fee in full during the first lesson and was always early for her lessons. After two lessons her dog was doing well with the training and she was very excited because she could again walk her dog, something that she had stopped doing because he was about 90 pounds and hard to handle if dogs walked by them.

I realized we were going to have a problem when she canceled her third lesson by emailing me just 15 minutes before the lesson was to start. She lives a 50 minute drive from my facility so that tells me that she was mentally debating if she was going to come and then at the last moment she decided she couldn't overcome her conflict. I emailed her back, suggesting that we meet up to just chat, she didn't even have to bring her dog if she didn't want to. She did show up for the session, thanking me for trying to make the process easier for her. 2 hours before her next session she emailed me to cancel that lesson, suggesting that she was not having a good day. Her email went something like this. "Ted, I know it's last minute, but I just can't do this anymore. I feel like I've wasted my money by coming to you and I don't even feel like I know what or why we are training my dog. I talked to my therapist about things and she agrees with me. I know that I signed a contract saying that your company does not give refunds, but I really think that I wasted my money, I didn't even bring my dog to the last lesson."

When I received this email, I'll be honest, I rolled my eyes. I told her that I don't provide refunds and that I would help her train her dog but she needed to show up for her lessons. "You paid for unlimited access to my knowledge and expertise, and you are not taking me up on that advice. I'm about as up front with clients in the beginning as a rich guy who meets a beautiful woman at a bar and tells her "So here's the deal, I'm loaded but, if this leads to marriage, you'll have to sign a prenup."

I convinced that client to come in for another lesson. She came in and apologized for her previous cancellation and for trying to blame her issues on me. I thank her for her honesty and we had a great lesson. Given the client's email suggestion that she didn't know what we were doing or why we were doing it, I had prepared a basic document for her and printed out several copies for her addressing those concerns. She thanked me for the extra time that I had spent on her behalf and did some training with her dog around my dogs before sitting down again. I told her that the ball was in her court. Her dog had shown significant changes already and that I would help her for as long as she needed, but that she would need to book the lessons with me and show up for her lessons. That last lesson was 6 months ago and she has not taken me up on my offer to help her further.

This begs the question, should I have given her a refund? If so, a partial refund or a full refund? This client has received much of my time already and was made fully aware of the time investment that she would need to make to change her dog's behaviour. She was not rushed in to a sale, in fact the opposite. She was given incredible service despite not keeping up to her word. At the time I chose not to give her a refund because she knew what she was getting into and was trying to act like a victim. It's possible that she was a victim in another area of her life, but not in the way that I treated her. If she calls me in ten years, I will help her, but she needs to ask for help.

Each of these situations is case by case. If you run group classes, you'll have clients who ask for refunds because they have to work late and can't make it to all of the lessons. If you do private lessons, you'll have clients who want a refund because they don't want to change or do any work. If you provide board and train programs you'll have clients who allow the dog to come home, and never do the daily maintenance training and then want a refund. It's impossible to entirely avoid refund requests, but with the correct education process early in the sales process, you can eliminate 95% of these requests.

IF YOU WANT to check out my free video course for dogs trainers you can check it out here: www.tedsbooks.com/book-2-res

BOARD AND TRAINS ARE NOT MY CUP OF TEA

*I*f you don't already know what a board and train is, it's when a dog trainer takes a dog into their home or facility and the trainer trains the dog, and then trains the owner to take over the training process. It's not my objective to deter any trainers from doing board and train programs because I know that some trainers love training dogs in this way, but keep reading because you might find this chapter enlightening.

WHAT ARE some of the good things about board and trains?
- The dog will get consistent training multiple times each day while they are with the trainer
- The client can have some time away from their dog if they are feeling overwhelmed
- You can train the dog on your own time, without feeling self conscious with the client watching

WHAT ARE some of the not so good things about board and trains?
- Personally I don't want to have to clean up explosive diarrhea at 4am if a dog is feeling under the weather

- It's likely to stress out your family members who live with you
- It's going to stress your own dogs
- It likely makes less money than if I were to do private lessons
- I don't want the liability
- It can be hard to say goodbye if you really like the dog
- Some trainers I know have had clients never pick up their dog, resulting in an awkward situation for the trainer and dog
- Most trainers report having far more issues with board and train clients after training as opposed to private lessons
- Most people don't want to be away from their dogs overnight

RATHER THAN GOING on a 10 page rant about why I don't like board and trains, I've decided to rather focus my thoughts on a few misconceptions about board and trains.

I'LL MAKE MORE money doing board and trains

This is just not true. Sure a bigger program price looks appetizing, but in reality when you break it down by the hour, you can make far more money doing private lessons. Have you ever recorded how many hours you invest in a board and train and how many hours you invest in a regular client who's doing private lessons? Let's do some math. The average trainer needs to invest about 5 hours each day into a board and train dog. Walking, training, and feeding takes a lot of time. If the trainer is doing a 2 week board and train for $2000, they are being paid $28 per hour that they invest in that dog.

They will also need to do a drop off lesson and a take home lesson. Add to that ongoing training to the client, and the time it took the trainer to write out detailed homework. Don't forget the daily emails and photos they sent to the client. In reality, the trainer who thinks they are making a killing doing board and trains is really making about $20/ hour.

$20/ hour is nothing to laugh at but when you do the math on private training or group classes, the numbers don't look so appetizing. My average program costs $1800. $200 goes to an e-collar that I include, and 15% goes to the tax man. So let's break down the numbers. $1330 is left after tools and tax. I typically spend about 6 hours with clients before transitioning them to group classes. My group classes on average consume about 2 hours per client per year. So for 8 hours invested, I'm making about $166/ hour by doing private lessons.

I have the most incredible setup at my facility for doing board and trains and I still don't like doing them because I don't like the liability, it doesn't pay very well, and I believe that the dogs and clients are better served by private lessons.

YOU CAN'T TRAIN *hard dogs unless you do it in a board and train*

Nope, this is not true. Trainers come from around the world to my shadow program and this is one of the most common things that they want to see. They don't believe that I can turn around aggressive dogs in private lessons. All of these shadow students see how I do things when they come to train with me. Nothing is hidden from the client at all, or the shadow students. If you need to take a dog in for a board and train because you have to do something so uncomfortable to the dog that you couldn't fathom having the skills during the training, I would highly suggest that you look deeper into your training abilities. Surely there are times in which I need to allow some dogs to go through some things that are uncomfortable in the name of personal change. Not all training can be 100% stress free, but the idea that you need to do anything behind closed doors is just wrong on so many levels. If you are feeling inadequate about your training abilities, feel free to email me personally and maybe I can help you with your training programs and techniques. ted@tedsbooks.com

DID you know that I help dog trainers with their businesses? If you are not yet a dog trainer and want an in-depth mentorship with me, go to: www.mangodogs.com/the-next-generation

. . .

IF YOU ALREADY HAVE A BUSINESS AND just want to come and work with me on your business for 10 days I have a program for that too! www. mangodogs.com/shadowted

DON'T ASSUME THAT ALL RESCUES
ARE GOOD TO HUMANS

*F*or a long time, I've been helping rescues with dogs, and in that time I've learned an incredible amount about how to approach these situations and how not to approach them. Most dog rescues will screw you over if you allow them to. As I read back that sentence I'm struck with how offensive those words sound, but it doesn't make them any less true. The boundaries that you set up, or don't set up will be the difference between a long-lasting relationship or an explosive failure. Many of the same tactics that I mentioned in the chapter about boundaries can be implemented with rescues, however, there are a lot of differences between clients relationships and rescue relationships.

IN THE VERY LEAST, you need to communicate these topics with rescues before starting a relationship;

- COMPENSATION
  - Tools and methodology
  - How many dogs you are willing to help
  - Which dogs you will and will not help

- Ongoing support
- Veterinarian care and feeding
- Liability
- Private lessons or do they come to live with you?

COMPENSATION

Many trainers help rescues, out of the goodness of their hearts, and others want to be paid for their time. Whatever you decide is up to you, but I have never been paid for helping. If you do not get paid for your help, one great hack that you can do is to be compensated with a tax break. If you align yourself with a registered rescue organization that is registered as a non-profit organization, they can give you a receipt that you can claim against your business taxes for the work that you did for the rescue. In essence you're not being paid upfront for your services with cash, however, at the end of the year, you will be given a deduction from your taxes because of the service that you provided for the organization. The rescue that I've worked most with unfortunately is not a registered nonprofit and so I don't get any tax deduction but I'm ok with that fact because I believe in what the organization is doing and I'm glad to help out. Other trainers charge the rescues their full training fee, and other trainers give the rescues a discount, so you'll need to decide what you are comfortable with before working with a rescue.

TOOLS AND METHODOLOGY

Early in my career, I was thrown under the bus by a dog rescue. They knew that I'm a balanced trainer and knew that some of their rescue supporters would not be happy about the rescue having me help out but they got stuck with a dog that was floating around from rescue to rescue. His name was Dewey, a dog who would redirect on people while on a leash if he saw another dog. Dewey also had an extensive history of dog aggression. The rescue contacted me saying that none of the other trainers in my city would help out, so I agreed to help Dewey, with the understanding that I would use a balanced approach. They had no more options and Dewey was days away from his euthanization appointment, so they agreed to the terms and dropped him off.

In 4 weeks he was a totally different dog and I found him a home with a local friend who owned a dog boarding facility. I showed everyone the process on my Facebook page as thousands around North America watched and applauded the process. After placing Dewey in his new home the rescue lost most of their financial donors and they started to claim that they had no idea that I was a balanced trainer. They lied to everyone and suggested that I had lied to them and told them that I was going to use an exclusively positive training protocol.

Before taking Dewey I had the rescue founder sign a contract highlighting all of the tools and techniques that I was going to use. I never did release that signed contract to the public in my defense. Just weeks after pointing the finger at me, the rescue closed its doors for lack of funding. What I learned in that situation was that rescues are run by good well-meaning people, but funding or lack of funding can cause them to make bad decisions when they are squeezed by the people who fund them. These days I only work with rescues that don't need funding to survive. Many local rescues saw what happened to me, and to the rescue that backstabbed me, so they know the gravity of what can happen when they align themselves with a balanced trainer.

About three years ago I started to take a slightly different approach to taking rescued dogs in for training. Now we put out a call to all trainers in our area, by way of the rescue's social media platforms. The rescue tags all of the local trainers on the post to ensure that everyone sees the post, and then they put out a video about the dog that needs training. They ask for help from any trainer regardless of the training style before they do any training with the dog. Unfortunately, they never get any of the trainers asking to help out with aggressive dogs, and so I step up and help the dog. If you are a balanced trainer, this is a good way to mitigate the potential harm the rescue might incur by using your services. If all trainers are notified that help is needed, and the dog is scheduled to be euthanized, how can anyone create an issue for the rescue? No more drama, no more loss of funding, and another dog saved.

How MANY DOGS you are willing to help

It's easy to wake up one morning and look around and see a house full of dogs. If that's the life that you want, and your spouse is ok with that, then fill your boots, but it's not the life that I want. 2-3 dogs is all that I want in my life because I feel suffocated when I have four or more dogs to care for. I was lucky that I put my foot down early in my years helping with rescues, letting them know that I was not going to take more than one dog at a time and that I would need at least one month off in between each dog that I helped with. Most of all I don't want to burden my wife. My wife is beautiful, talented, and an amazing mother but she's not a crazy dog lady. She likes dogs but doesn't want a house full of them, and so I decided the moment I proposed to her that I would not allow myself to say yes to any dog if it would jeopardize my marriage. She's been a good sport lover over the years and has always been very accommodating of my interest in dogs, but I refuse to take advantage of her.

Outline how many dogs you will take at a time, and stipulate that you will need recovery time so that you can decompress in between dogs. Make your dogs, and your spouse the priority over the dogs that need help, because if you don't, you might wake up one day to an empty spot next to you in your bed. Rescues are famous for making dog trainers feel bad about not taking dogs. They are amazing at it, and it's terrible because it doesn't help anyone. When they push dogs on trainers, they are thinking short term. It doesn't help the dogs because these trainers get overwhelmed and just stop taking dogs, and then the rescue is down one trainer, and many dogs are turned away.

The rescues that I work with know that if they call me and say "He's got nowhere else to go" that I will help if I have time and space, but they will get a quick and confident no if I don't have time or space. This may seem cold but I'm happily married and only have dogs in my home that I chose to be there, and I'm not resentful to anyone for taking advantage of me because I don't let people manipulate me into helping when it's not a good time for my family.

WHICH DOGS you will and will not take

Knowing the dogs that you will enjoy working with, helping, and learning from is important. Knowing which dogs are going to drive you insane is also key to a long career helping rescue dogs. I absolutely loathe working with dogs with extreme separation anxiety but I love working with aggressive dogs. Dogs who struggle with advanced separation anxiety or containment phobia are an insane amount of work and will cause me to lose a lot of sleep. I'm not a great person to be around when I'm tired, I'm cranky and I'm prone to saying disrespectful things to the people around me when I'm not well-rested. This is why I don't take dogs with separation anxiety. It's a massive stress on my marriage. Communicate with the rescue that you work with and let them know about types of dogs that you want to work with and the dogs that you don't want to work with. If you don't like working with aggressive dogs, then don't allow them to send you any. Do what you are good at and enjoy, and don't allow any dog rescue to pressure you into doing anything that you don't want to do.

ONGOING SUPPORT

When working with rescue dogs it's important that the rescue has a plan set up for each dog that is in their system. Dogs that need a trainer, also need a foster and a forever home that will provide ongoing support and training. Rescues only place dogs that need expensive medications with people who have the financial resources to buy those dogs medications, and they should do the same with dogs that need ongoing training. It's been very natural for me to integrate these rescue dogs into my weekly group classes that I already do for my clients so that fosters and adopters have ongoing support. Why train any dog if the dog does not have access to ongoing support to solidify their skills over the long term? When I work with rescue dogs, I will only take the dog if I'm able to supply ongoing free support to the new home. Why free? Anything with a financial obligation can be a hindrance for people who rescue a dog. Countless times I've had people call me telling me that they recently adopted a new dog from another local rescue organization and they were unwilling to invest any money into this new dog.

Anyone who's worked in rescue knows that the first four weeks are critical to a dog staying in their home because most dogs are returned in that time due to behavioural issues. The first weeks are often fun for the owners because they have a new dog in their home and the novelty of their new addition is still present much like the honeymoon period for humans in a new relationship. Of course, some of these newly adopted dogs will start to change their behaviour shortly after settling into their new homes and that can be a problem that costs a dog their life. Common behavioural issues are the largest reason why dog owners surrender their dogs in the first place, and if the goal is to keep as many of these dogs in their homes forever, ongoing training is essential.

I offer unlimited free training to all of my dog training clients, so I can help my clients keep their results over the lifetime of their dog. If you don't already provide group classes, I would suggest setting up a free group walk once a week in a local neighbourhood. Make a basic page on your website that has all of the information for your classes and give it out to people who are adopting a dog that you have worked with. Don't send out emails to people as reminders because most of them will go to their spam folders. Give them the link and tell them to bookmark the page on their smartphones and computers so they can check the class schedule before coming out. This little website trick has saved me countless hours in sending hundreds of thousands of emails over the years. Don't have anywhere to do your classes? Pick a random Walmart parking lot and get started. Have them meet in the parking lot and go for a group walk together. After the walk, you can answer any questions they might have about their dogs' behaviour. Remember that training the rescue dog is only the first battle. Keeping the dog's behavior up to date is just as important.

. . .

Veterinarian care and feeding

As the trainer, you'll want to be sure that you are not getting stuck with having to pay for Vet care or the feeding of any rescue dogs that you are working with. Rescues always have resources for both of these, and it should be their responsibility to ensure that you have everything that you need to keep the dog you are working with in a healthy physical shape. The internet is a wonderful help in fundraising and I've seen countless rescues raise over $10,000 in one day for a dog that needed extensive surgery. Ask your rescue if they have funds to provide food and Vet care. If the dog will be living with you during training, ask if the rescue has someone working in the organization that can drop off the food to you so that you don't have to go and pick up dog food. The more streamlined they can make the process for you, the more dogs you will be able to help. The rescue should make your job as easy as possible so that you can do your best work with the dog that is in need.

Liability, and who owns the rescue dog?

If I could only write one sentence on this entire dog trainer/rescue topic I would say this. *Don't give rescues the opportunity to leave dogs with you without signing some critical contracts.* Over the years I've seen many of my friends be left with abandoned dogs after rescues shut down their doors. You need to legally specify which dates you will be working with the dog and when they will pick up the dog after training. Also, note in your contract that you're not taking legal responsibility or ownership of the dog. These simple little tricks are the only reason that I still have a house full of dogs that I 100% selected to be in my home. My dogs are incredible, and I never have to look at them as a burden because I allowed a rescue to take advantage of my generosity.

Private lessons or do they come to live with you?

Up until this point, I have assumed that you will be taking the rescue dog in as a board and train student. This is how most trainers work with these dogs because these dogs do not yet have homes. You could also have them live with a foster while you help with the training. Doing this requires a good foster that is willing to invest a lot of time each day into training. While I have met a few of these fosters in the past, these fosters do not tend to be the norm. Unless your rescue organization can find fosters that will put in the time and work, it's best to offer a board and train option if you have room in your home for such cases.

If you have a soft spot for helping dogs in need, I commend you for your empathy but remember that your empathy could turn you bitter if you don't protect yourself when working with rescues and shelters. When I look back on all of the rescue dogs that I've helped I can honestly say that it has been very rewarding, and I hope the same for you.

If you want to check out my free video course for dogs trainers you can check it out here: www.tedsbooks.com/book-2-res

DO LESS, MAKE MORE

*I*f you are currently a one-person business, you are not alone. Most dog training businesses are run by one trainer who runs the entire business. This one-person business has plenty of benefits associated with it. If given the choice between having to pay one salary every two weeks or numerous salaries, it's easy to figure out why so many dog trainers decide to keep their businesses small.

If you are a dog trainer and think that you need staff, allow me to suggest a few other options before we assume that you need staff. I've had staff in the past and found it to be more of a bother than an asset. As I look back on those hires, I realize that I was just self-medicating my busyness, convincing myself that having staff would increase profits and allow me to take more time off. I no longer believe that lie, because I now have plenty of free time, am making more money than ever and I have no staff at all. This chapter focuses on how I stopped doing meaningless things that were wasting countless hours. A chapter less about *what I do* to be productive, and more about *what I don't do.*

Personally, I don't think that you need to have a staff to run a great dog training business, make great money, and have leftover time to enjoy your dogs, friends, and family. I run a dog training business that makes over $100,000 a year, and yet I can still make my wife, dogs and kids a priority. I still have enough time to write 4 books a year, take every Sunday off of work, and travel the world doing seminars. I do absolutely everything apart from proofreading the books and editing the audiobooks which I outsource to people in Europe for a small cost. To that, I should add that I pay an accountant to handle my books because the thought of numbers makes my head explode.

Before assuming that you need staff, let's see if we can save you something like 20 hours a week. If we can do that, you can invest that time however you like. You can invest that time into training dogs to make a profit, or take some time off, it's up to you. The process will look at just a few things like emails, social media, phone calls and marketing.

ELIMINATING unneeded operational inefficiencies

If the goal is to work less and make more, the answer is not always to hire staff or even to outsource to virtual staff. One of my favorite books is the 4 hour work week written by Timothy Ferris and the largest single takeaway that I learned from that book is to eliminate things from your business that are not needed.

How many hours a day do you spend in your email inbox and on social media? Do you know? How many times do you check your email per day? How many times do you go on Facebook or Instagram? When I message many of my dog trainer friends on Facebook, I get a response within 10 minutes. What that tells me is that their phone buzzed to let them know that someone was seeking them, so they responded quickly to a message that's not an emergency. When people message me, they will typically get a response in 24 hours as I only go on Facebook once a day.

IT'S MUCH MORE **beneficial to batch all of these responses. If you have a smartphone, turn off all notifications now. They are costing you thousands of dollars in lost productivity.**

. . .

IF YOU WASTE 3 hours a day continually caught up in an email and social media, the solution is not to hire staff because you are too busy, the answer is to fix your wasting of time so that you can focus on tasks that actually move the needle for your business. You could swap out 3 hours of needless email, social media, and texting, with billable hours that could easily increase your yearly income by $20,000 or more. It's astounding what one can accomplish when they are focused. Don't live your life in defense, live your life in offense.

Email is defensive in nature and you can think of it as another person's expectations for your day. The good news is that you can cut your email time down by 80% or more in just a few days. Your first step will be to batch your email. By batching I'm suggesting only looking at your emails once or twice a day at the most. If you think that you'll lose business to your competitors you are probably overreacting. When people call, it's usually more urgent, so don't stress over the emails because when people email a business, they expect to wait at least 24 hours to get a response. Your next step will be to set up an auto-responder on your email account that automatically responds to emails with a response. Something simple like "Hey, thanks for sending me an email, your email is important to me, but I only have time to get to my emails once per day. I will email you back within 24 hours or less. Thanks and have a great day! If you struggle with email or social media withdrawals like most do when attempting a digital detox, start with allowing yourself to indulge 4 times a day, then 3, then 2. I've found that the sweet spot is 1-2 times per day for optimal productivity without losing potential clients.

Next will be to unsubscribe to any emails that you don't want to clog up your email account. If it's not directly business related and important, you should not be allowing it to hit your email inbox. When you check your email and it's got 30 new emails, you will be more likely to feel overwhelmed, which is why you should keep your email clear from unneeded alerts that only serve to clutter your inbox and create the illusion of an overwhelming task. Don't keep email tabs open on your computer unless you are specifically responding to emails. If your eye sees that there is a new email, you will be more likely to stop what you are doing and address that email.

It might not seem like much but every time that you stop a task to start a new task, you lose concentration and you waste time. If I had my email open while writing this book, I would constantly be fighting the urge to check those emails, and so I don't give my brain access to being distracted. It's for the same reason that I don't keep potato chips in my house, I don't want to be tempted into eating them.

Your next step will be to determine if you should be emailing or texting with clients about subjects that are better addressed over the phone. I don't know about you but I can address most dog training questions in a 5-7 minute phone conversation when that might take me 10-15 emails back and forth with the client to achieve the same amount of learning and communication. Email requires that the sender must wait for a response before they can clarify. If I get a question over email that is training related, more often than not I will pick up the phone and call the client. In the past I've watched myself get involved in a back and forth email thread that took 6 emails from the sender and 6 emails from the receiver, just to book a time for a lesson. What an extreme waste of time. Don't waste days or weeks going back and forth over text or email if you can clarify the issue with a quick phone call.

The next step is to take note of why your clients or potential clients are emailing you most often. What questions do you get on an almost daily basis? If you want to cut down on the number of emails that you get exponentially, you should take note of these questions and do a better job at answering these questions before they come up. If you consistently get questions about when your next set of classes is starting, you could address this by setting up an auto-responder that says something like "Hey, thanks for your email. Your email is important to me! I'm with clients right now and only get the opportunity to check my emails once every 24 hours. If you are interested in signing up to one of our upcoming obedience classes, you can see find out more information, and even sign up on our website. www.123dogtraining.com/classes

If you need something else that I can help you with, just email me back and I'll get back to you as soon as I possibly can." A simple email like this can reduce your emails by 50% if you do a lot of basic obedience or puppy classes.

If you are not already asking every person who contacts you how they came to hear about your company, you need to start doing that as soon as possible. Every person who fills out the contact form on my website must. If they fill out that form and I talk to them on the phone, I can ask them over the phone. If you do meet with these people in person, be sure to ask them when you sit down with them. Create a spreadsheet, or use a paper notebook to keep your data in one place. Now let's look at how potential clients have come to hear about my company in the last year;

- Google search: 53%
- Friend Referral: 27%
- Facebook: 9%
- Vet referral: 6%
- Other: 5%
- Youtube: 0%

Social media seems to have a bigger effect on some dog trainers businesses than others. As you can see, Facebook, the only social platform that I use is not even in the double digits. For me it's a waste of time, but I continue to use Facebook because it helps me sell books and online courses. Facebook might be a waste of time for you. Don't just assume that because everyone uses it, that it's a great investment in your time. I say this because I've run the numbers and I'm currently scaling back from social media channels and investing my time and advertising budget in other, more profitable channels.

In the past, I was on Facebook, Twitter, Instagram, and Youtube. Currently, I only use Facebook and youtube. Youtube has never brought me a client, so I only use it to host videos for my website. While my Facebook page gets a lot of traffic and helps sell books, it does very little to bring in new clients. As you can see Google search is working, so I'm investing heavily into writing blogs and paying a search engine optimization company to help with my Google ranking.

If you're interested in that company, I use www.thehoth.com for my search engine work.

Referrals have always been a big help to my business, so I note when a client refers someone to my business. If I get a referral from a past client, I will email that client to thank them for the referral. Once a year, I send all of my clients a postcard in the mail. The cards are made at Staples business depot and are very cheap to print; the postage costs more than the card! This card has a photo of my dogs on one side and on the other side there is a photo of me and my dogs with some text that says "Thanks for trusting me to train your dog, and thanks for the referrals, all the best in the New Year!" Few people send things in the mail these days, so it's a great way to place yourself at the top of your past clients' minds. Many clients put the card on their refrigerator because of the nice photos of my dogs on the card. Doing little things like this actually helps to keep you at the top of people's minds, so go ahead and make up some cards for your clients!

Investing time and money trying to market your business in ways that are not working is an incredible waste of resources. In my first book, "Thriving Dog Trainers", I suggest that trainers should not invest time into doing daily Facebook videos if they are not getting any traction. Just because it's free to post a short video on Facebook every day, it's a waste of time if you are not getting clients from it. Few dog trainers have enough skills and confidence to do a good job at posting the video on Facebook. I know a handful that have mastered it, but most are just wasting precious time. For others, maybe a better use of their time would be to write articles about dog training and use keywords that get your page seen on Google.

Clearly I'm not against video, or Facebook for that matter, but I can't help but be stunned by the numbers. Most of my clients come from referrals and Google. Is it smart for me to invest a lot of time or money into Facebook if it's not really moving the needle? I have over 5500 people on my Facebook page and it still brings such an insignificant amount of clients my way. If this is not true for you, and Facebook is bringing in a huge amount of clients for you, I'd love to hear what you are doing, so shoot me an email at ted@tedsbooks.com.

. . .

DID you know that I help dog trainers with their businesses? If you are not yet a dog trainer and want an in-depth mentorship with me, go to: www.mangodogs.com/the-next-generation

IF YOU ALREADY HAVE A BUSINESS AND just want to come and work with me on your business for 10 days I have a program for that too! www.mangodogs.com/shadowted

DO YOU NEED STAFF?

In the previous chapter I don't hold back on my aversion to having staff. I just don't see the need for most dog trainers to have a staff. Let it be known that I'm not an authority in the area of staffing and for that reason I reached out to a brilliant mind to help write the next chapter on hiring staff. Unless I've been in the trenches, I don't like to talk as though I have. I've only had two staff members at my company and neither of those staff was resounding successes in making my business more profit or giving me back significant amounts of time.

REASONS why you might want to have staff;

- You don't like working alone
- You have a retail store portion to your business and need someone to be in the building during regular business hours
- You do a large volume of dog training clients and need other trainers to help

THE NEGATIVES TO HAVING STAFF;

- It creates additional competition for you if they leave the business and start their own business nearby
- If you are not great at delegating tasks, you will not free up more time for yourself
- Two or more salaries need to be paid in lean months

MY EXPERIENCE with staff in my business has not been terrible, but more of a bother than anything. Of all of my friends who are trainers who have had staff, the majority of them let the staff go and went back to being single operators like myself after 6-12 months. Before talking about making your first full time hire, let's talk about another great hiring option, outsourcing.

Why hire staff when you can rent staff? Outsourcing is an incredible alternative to hiring staff unless you absolutely need to hire staff as a trainer or kennel staff. Unless you need someone in your physical location, it's unlikely that you need regular staff. One area where outsourcing can be incredible is when you have things in your business that absolutely need to be done but you hate doing them or literally can't do them. If you absolutely hate doing your taxes, then hire someone to do your taxes. Many of the dog trainers that I know hate answering their phones, and that's something that you can easily outsource to a virtual assistant.

If you've already freed up countless hours and still find yourself to be too busy to meet the demand, you can do a few things before hiring full-time staff. You could increase your prices which in turn will allow you to make more money and work less. If fewer people sign up for your services, that's ok, because you will need fewer clients to make the same amount of money or more. Personally, I don't have staff and only work with about 70 clients per year. I'm making more money now then I was when I was working with 120 clients per year. How is that possible? Be known to be the best of the best in your local area at one thing, and then charge the price that you want to charge for your time. If too many of your potential clients tell you that your prices are too high, lower them by 20%. I'm able to be 100% with my clients because I'm not overburdened by having a massive overflow of clients that I feel I need to service. Sometimes doing less is more. It's my experience after coaching dog trainers around the world, most dog trainers are afraid to raise their prices, and so they keep them the same and hire a staff instead. When this happens, most or all of that profit is eaten up by the new staff salary and they are right back to where they were before.

If you have your heart set on having a staff, you'll want to decide whether you should hire an administrative staff or a dog trainer as staff. And before doing so, you should always hire staff on a part-time or seasonal basis. Kayla was my first hire, and she was incredible at her job. She had worked in administration before and was also great at graphic design and photography. She was told that she would have full-time hours and a great salary, but that she would be working alone. Her job title included all the emails, most of the phone calls, organizing my group classes, my social media posts and would walk my dogs if I was too busy to walk them some days.

All was great for the first few months until she started to talk about being bored. We had discussed that she would have her own office, but she would be working alone, and clearly, she had underestimated how much she needed colleagues near her each day. After six months, we reached the Christmas season which for me each year is always a slow season. We sat down to talk about her taking a few weeks off work and she decided to get a job in a chiropractic clinic so that she could work closer to people. I'm fortunate to have had her work with me because she taught me about graphic design, but also because I learned that I don't need full-time staff. I learned that I could eliminate or outsource almost everything that she did for me.

If I was too busy to walk my dogs once a week, I could pay the dog walker down the street $25 to take them out. I got serious about learning how to minimize my emails, and so now I spend almost no time in my inbox anymore. My website now helps to minimize getting too many phone calls and emails. These days I'm working even less, making more, and I have no staff.

My next and final experience with hiring was with Joe. Joe had been a contact person with a local dog rescue and had been bringing in dogs for evaluation when they came into Canada. I liked Joe and he was very eager to learn about dog behaviour and aggression. After coming over a few times, we became friends and he started dropping in to hang out and train dogs with me. In those days, Joe was working as an audio engineer and was at the top of his field but he wanted a change. After the company that employed him for many years went bankrupt, we talked about him coming on as a part-time trainer. I was candid with Joe when I told him that he would have to open his own business so that I could hire him as a contractor. The paperwork required to have Kayla on staff was not something that I wanted to allow back into my life, so hiring Joe as a contractor was a smart idea in simplifying our business relationship. Joe worked with me for a few years but left the business after being offered 50% ownership at no cost if he helped open a doggy daycare. For Joe, this was a great move and the location was only 5 minutes from his home. He's still one of my best friends in the world and I'm happy to watch him grow and develop as an entrepreneur.

If I had to go back and change things with Kayla, I don't think that I would because I learned a lot about what not to do. Don't hire someone full time, when no position is really needed. Don't hire admin before you have streamlined your business and have really done the work to eliminate as much admin work from your business as you possibly can. If your staff is going to have to work alone for most of the day, start them out on a trial basis before giving them a full-time job. If I had to do it again, I would have started her on a part-time basis and would have had her start her own small business so that I could pay her as a contractor, which would not have forced me to file extra taxes and employee paperwork.

Looking back I don't think that I did anything wrong with Joe. I was careful to eliminate the extra paperwork and taxes as Joe had set himself up as a small business. Joe was also told that I would send him all of my puppy clients and basic obedience clients, but that he would have to do his own marketing if he wanted to be busy 6 days a week. If he was not willing to go out to dog parks and veterinarians, this job was not for him. That took the weight of having to keep him busy all of the time off of my shoulders.

After having both an admin staff and a trainer staff, I realize that I had to fill both positions to show myself that I was wrong about needing staff. They didn't make my business more profitable, or really make my life easier in any significant ways. I was convinced that an admin would make my life easier until I realized that I could eliminate most of that work and not have to pay anyone every two weeks. I took on Joe because he was a friend and he told me that he would help me with my weekly group classes. Well, I never needed that help because after he left the company I increased my prices again and I have fewer dogs in my weekly classes now which I can easily handle on my own. Less can be more.

With both Kayla and Joe, I had very specific expectations lined out for them before they started. I refer to these things as the "things that will get you fired" list. Before hiring a staff member, sit down and I give them a list of things that will get them fired. Some of these infractions will get them fired on the first infraction, and others will require 3 or 5 to be fired. For example, if my trainer were to physically hit a dog they would be immediately fired. If they showed up late for work, they would have 4 infractions before being fired. Every time that trainer does something that is on the list, they have to sign and date your copy of the company policies.

This infraction list is often used in doggy daycares to keep track of how many times a staff member has left gates open. Leaving a gate open in a daycare could result in a dog getting outside and being hit by a car, so the stakes are high. Keeping track of these things is important to minimize the potential of the staff member coming back in the future and insisting that they had a blemish-free track record. Not having these conversations early is like getting married and not discussing where you are going to live or if you want to have children or not.

IF YOU WANT to check out my free video course for dogs trainers you can check it out here: www.tedsbooks.com/book-2-res

WHEN HIRING STAFF

For this section, I reached out to my friend Tyler Muto because he's a really great trainer and owns a dog training facility in Buffalo NY with 10 full-time staff. Tyler has much more knowledge in the area of hiring so I chatted with him for an hour and he imparted some timeless hiring principles. Thanks, Tyler!

TYLER TOLD me that he hired staff for three reasons.

1. He wanted to build a medium-sized business that someday he could sell
2. He wanted to build a business that would make money even if he didn't show up to work or went on vacation
3. He wanted a facility that not only produced well-trained dogs and happy clients, but he also wanted grooming and daycare to be available for his clients

HE TOLD me that he didn't really like the day-to-day grind of having to train clients from start to finish, but he much prefers his role of stopping in each day to help his staff learn to be better trainers. He prefers the role of a coach over being the business owner. His job is to provide vision to the company and coach his staff in ways that help them flourish as trainers.

I asked him when a trainer should look for staff and what role they should have and he was adamant that business owners should hire staff to do the stuff that they don't like to do, the things you don't have time to do and to hire for their weaknesses. He thinks it's important to hire first for administrative staff if you want to spend more time training or hire a trainer first if you want to spend more time working on the business. "If you hate being on the phone, hire someone to do that." As his business grew, he added admin staff and trainers, and then he added daycare staff and kennel workers to round out his business.

A FEW LESSONS that he learned along the way;

- Don't hire friends to work for you
- Don't get too friendly with your staff
- It's very important to get good at hiring, but it's equally as important to know when to terminate staff
- Have a clear job description for staff before they start
- Have regular performance reviews with staff
- You can incentivize some staff with money, but others would prefer a title, others prefer positive feedback from leadership, others gratitude. A combination is best
- Be sure to keep your staff connected with the broader story of the business. Forward positive emails from your clients to staff so that they know how appreciated they are, or email them a screenshot if they get a positive review on Facebook or Google
- Make an active effort to find things to praise staff for!

WHAT TYPES of things should you look for in staff?

- Character is a big thing
- Has good morals
- Good work ethic
- Eager to learn
- Eager to be part of a team
- Communication skills
- Self-directed

THINGS THAT ARE RED FLAGS;

- If they clearly don't fit in with the business owner, the rest of the staff or your clients
- Complaining
- Expecting things (entitled view on life)
- Not willing to take direction or feedback
- If they talk slanderously about past jobs

TYLER TELLS his staff to come to him with big questions because he does a great job showing his staff what they should be doing and leaving them alone to do it. "Don't micromanage people, they hate that!" Show them the goal, tell them what they can do, and tell them what they cannot do, give them a time constraint and then walk away and let them get to work.

SOME WORDS OF WISDOM;

- Learn how to delegate responsibilities to your staff or you will get stuck doing all of the work as you seek perfection

- Accept that no one is going to do it as well as you, you need to accept that
- Delegate to the person's strengths. You are not going to change people
- Praise in public, reprimand in private
- He makes his trainers sign a non-competition document, but does not make his other staff sign one
- You must have employee manuals so that they know what they are supposed to do and what they are not supposed to do
- He pays his managers on a salary and his employees are paid an hourly wage

TYLER THOUGHT it would be important to caution newer trainers about hiring staff and especially leasing a facility. "As you start making money, you start to think that more staff and more space will solve your problems. You don't necessarily need staff or a facility. When you hire staff you take on a massive responsibility to those employees, particularly if they have families at home to provide for. As you grow, you are creating a machine and that machine needs to be fed. Think long and hard before you sign a lease or hire staff to help you in your business, and be sure to do it one step at a time."

CHECK OUT TYLER'S website for loads of great dog training videos that will help you take your craft to the next level! www. considerthedog.com

WHEN FIRING STAFF

*I*t's not hard to imagine how difficult it would be to fire or lay off an employee. If you've never had to be a part of this unpleasant task, it's just plain terrible. Inevitably you will have made some sort of a bond with your employee and it's always hard to disappoint people even if your business is suffering because they are on your team. I have had to fire staff in the past in previous businesses and I definitely learned an incredible amount about what not to do from those situations.

When will you know that it's time to fire or lay someone off? Laying off an employee is much easier if you know when your business has slow seasons, and this only comes with time and experience. It's common for dog trainers to be given the month of December off of work because there is simply not enough work to go around unless you are a puppy trainer. You'll know when the slow seasons are so that you can prepare your staff for those seasons. Knowing when to terminate a staff member is a little like knowing when to get out of a relationship, there is no specific time, but there is a breaking point. I personally think that having a well-defined code of conduct which I mentioned in the previous chapter is the best possible way to define when the staff has broken enough rules to call it quits. If you have a loose rule like; don't be late, your staff could be late 50 times in a year and you might never have a specific moment to look back to when thinking about firing them.

When a staff member is causing your business to lose money or is bringing a lot of drama into your business, you need to let them go. Destroying your company culture only takes one staff member. Having a toxic person on staff is harder to regulate because it's hard to measure mood and words. In your code of conduct, you can list things like talking ill about other trainers, swearing, yelling, as potential issues that can be recorded, but really at the end of the day; you will know a toxic energy in someone when you see it.

When your gut has told you three times that you need to let someone go, you need to just pull the bandaid off and do it. The longer you wait, the worse off everyone will be.

Putting new staff on a trial period is a great way to get to know people before you hire them. I would take it even one step further and suggest asking people to work for free for a few weeks to see if they are a good fit. Admin staff or kennel staff might not be willing to do this because it's two weeks in which they are not being paid, but if a potential trainer wants it badly enough they would take the job and work for free. I know that when I was starting out I would have slept on broken glass for someone to help me become a better dog trainer.

The vast majority of the emotional pain that you will incur before firing someone is self-inflicted. By this I mean to say that there are things that I could have done earlier. Did you properly communicate your expectations with the staff before they started? Incomplete communication is the largest reason why it's hard to fire people because it's hard to indicate a specific moment where things went wrong.

One little tip that I think is key for business owners is to give staff specific direction on things that they like and things that they don't like. For example, I like when people show up for work 10 minutes early. I don't like when people show up to work 10 minutes late. I like when staff asks me for help if they need help, I don't like when staff don't ask for help and mess up with a client. Create a list for 20 likes and 20 dislikes that will help your staff know if they are doing a good job, or if they are aggravating you.

If you want to check out my free video course for dogs trainers you can check it out here: www.tedsbooks.com/book-2-res

IN CLOSING

$\mathcal{T}$he knowledge that I've shared with you is in large part ideas that I have learned by doing things incorrectly. Never be afraid to look back on your past mistakes and learn from them, just as I have. Don't forget to check out the free video course! www.tedsbooks.com/book-2-res

THANK YOU!

If you have questions, feel free to email me personally, I love helping out dog owners and trainers. Email: ted@tedsbooks.com.

DON'T FORGET to review the book on Amazon, it really helps me out!!! Thanks in advance.

- *Join the mailing list*
- *Find all of my other books*
- *Access online training sessions with me*

- *At www.tedsbooks.com*

DID you know that I help dog trainers with their businesses? If you are not yet a dog trainer and want an in-depth mentorship with me, go to: www.mangodogs.com/the-next-generation

IF YOU ALREADY HAVE A BUSINESS AND just want to come and work with me on your business for 10 days I have a program for that too! www.mangodogs.com/shadowted

ALSO BY TED EFTHYMIADIS

All titles are available on Amazon in Kindle and Physical book some, some are available in audiobook version from www.audible.com

Thriving Dog Trainers: An indispensable tool to help you start or repair your dog training business (Business books for dog trainers)

Giving Up On My Dog: A straightforward directive for those close to giving up on their dog

Prong Collar Training for Pet Dogs: The only resource you'll need to train your pet dog with the aid of a prong collar (Dog Training for Pet Dogs) (Volume 1)

Potty Training Puppy: A comprehensive guide to help you navigate the crappy job of house training your puppy

E-COLLAR TRAINING for Pet Dogs: The only resource you'll need to train your dog with the aid of an electric training collar (Dog Training for Pet Dogs)